I0125019

Exoneree

Exoneree

by *Uriah Courtney*

WITH *Glenda Faye Mathes*

FOREWORDS BY
Michael Horton and Justin Brooks

CASCADE *Books* · Eugene, Oregon

EXONEREE

Copyright © 2017 Uriah Courtney and Glenda Faye Mathes. All rights reserved. Except for brief quotations in critical publications or reviews, no part of this book may be reproduced in any manner without prior written permission from the publisher. Write: Permissions, Wipf and Stock Publishers, 199 W. 8th Ave., Suite 3, Eugene, OR 97401.

Cascade Books
An Imprint of Wipf and Stock Publishers
199 W. 8th Ave., Suite 3
Eugene, OR 97401

www.wipfandstock.com

PAPERBACK ISBN: 978-1-5326-1446-0
HARDCOVER ISBN: 978-1-5326-1448-4
EBOOK ISBN: 978-1-5326-1447-7

Cataloguing-in-Publication data:

Names: Courtney, Uriah, with Glenda Faye Mathes.

Title: Exoneree / Uriah Courtney with Glenda Faye Mathes.

Description: Eugene, OR: Cascade Books, 2017.

Identifiers: ISBN 978-1-5326-1446-0 (paperback) | ISBN 978-1-5326-1448-4 (hardcover) | ISBN 978-1-5326-1447-7 (ebook)

Subjects: LCSH: Courtney, Uriah. | Prisoners United States Biography. | Title.

Classification: HV9468 .C45 2017 (print) | HV9468 (ebook)

Manufactured in the U.S.A.   DECEMBER 1, 2017

Cover photo © David Brooks/San Diego Union-Tribune via ZUMA Wire

Unless otherwise indicated, all Scripture quotations are from the ESV© Bible (The Holy Bible, English Standard Version©), copyright © 2001 by Crossway, a publishing ministry of Good News Publishers. Used by permission. All rights reserved.

Table of Contents

TABLE OF CONTENTS

Two Reasons You Should Read This Book

WHAT WOULD I DO—AND how would I view the world around me—if I had been the victim of wrongful imprisonment? I have had the pleasure of meeting a number of inmates through the years who have experienced God's grace in Jesus Christ. They know something at a very deep and practical level about hearing verdicts: "guilty" and "not guilty." The reality of divine judgment and justification is often more easy to convey to those who have heard that sort of a verdict in a human courtroom.

Then there are others who speak of their "jailhouse conversions" for a variety of effects. One reason might be that it contributes a sense of exoneration from their past: I was the guy who ripped off the liquor store or embezzled the company's revenues, but not anymore. A lot of times it's true and a lot of times it's not. I think that many people who tell those stories believe them. It's just that they don't really understand the depths of sin and grace.

But it's something completely different when you are not guilty to begin with and have nevertheless heard a guilty verdict pronounced along with a prison sentence—in spite of the fact that you're not the right person.

I can't even imagine Uriah's trial of faith in the aftermath of his unjust conviction and sentence. Because human beings make mistakes, sometimes grievous ones like this, it makes sense. But what about God? Doesn't he know everything? Isn't he in control of all things? Doesn't he love me? And if he loves me and is all-powerful, how can this happen?

A shallow faith should lead one at that point to give up. If your deepest religious thought is how to have "your best life now," then obviously God is not worth the time or effort.

But then you go back into the history of God's dealings with his people. Thrown into a pit out of jealousy by his brothers, Joseph was sold into slavery in Egypt. Just when it looked as if he was crawling out of a dungeon,

vii

literally, the wife of a government official fingered him as a rapist because he wouldn't sleep with her. After a trial of errors, he became the prime minister of Egypt. When his brothers came begging to the court for basic necessities to take back home, Joseph revealed his identity. Of course, they were terrified. What would he do to them now? He was the most powerful person in Egypt next to the Pharaoh himself. And yet Joseph could say, "You meant it for evil, but God meant it for good, in order to save many people."

Have you ever seen a tapestry up close? Look at the threads on the back. A tangled web of string, right? Yes, until you turn it over and see the beautiful scene on the front. Our lives are often like that. From our perspective, life doesn't make sense. God doesn't make sense. But something far greater than we could have imagined emerges from the ordeals that he put us through. By making us a witness to his grace and power, he not only saves and comforts others but shakes us up so that we see things from his perspective rather than from our puny vistas of personal peace and affluence.

Uriah has gone through that Joseph-like experience to emerge at the other end as a witness to God's grace and glory. God is not for him a cosmic bellhop who owes him health, wealth, and happiness. Nor does Uriah pretend that because he's not guilty of the crime for which he was wrongly convicted he is acquitted in God's courtroom. He knows that we all deserve condemnation in that eternal tribunal, but he clings solely to the life and death of Jesus Christ in his place and to the Savior's resurrection as the guarantee of his own resurrection from the dead.

So the great story of the Bible—and the doctrines that arise from it—are not for Uriah something he takes for granted. He knows every day, perhaps in a way that he never experienced as fully, that he is chosen, redeemed, adopted, justified, and is being gradually made new in Jesus Christ by the power of the Holy Spirit—through faith alone.

Uriah's story has been of incredible encouragement to someone like me, far less touched by injustice. He has two important stories to tell here. The first is the warning that the best justice systems of human beings, whatever the admirable principles and processes, aren't perfect. Uriah's story provokes us to demand more faithful execution of our justice system as part of a larger debate that we need in our society today. But the most important lesson we have to learn from Uriah's story is that regardless of what our fellow sinners can do to us or even for us, our only comfort in life and in death is our faithful Savior Jesus Christ.

I hope that you will be as encouraged, enlightened, and emboldened as I have by the story Uriah tells here.

Dr. Michael Horton
J. Gresham Machen Professor of Systematic Theology and Apologetics
Westminster Seminary California

An Unforgettable Moment

I will never forget the day I was able to go to Donovan Prison and tell Uriah Courtney that DNA testing proved he was innocent of the crime he had spent eight years in prison for. Of course, he had always known he was innocent and I believed him, but a scientific test finally proved to the world that he was an innocent man. Uriah looked so vulnerable and so hopeful while he waited to hear why I'd come with the lawyers and law students who had worked on his case.

With a straight face, I told him, "You know I would be here only if I had good news or bad news."

"Yep," he answered.

I couldn't hold back my smile. "I've got really great news."

Then we all cried.

That was one of the greatest moments in my life. What could feel better than giving someone the news that they are going to get their life back after society has locked them up, thrown them away, and forgot about them? I gave Uriah a bear hug and could feel him shaking with emotions few of us will ever know.

Hard as it is to believe he spent over eight years in prison for a crime he didn't commit, it's true.

I've told Uriah how lucky he is, just as I've told the twenty-five other people the California Innocence Project has freed over the years. Uriah was lucky the evidence in his case had not been thrown out, lucky that it wasn't contaminated beyond the point of being testable, lucky we were able to get access to the DNA databank, and lucky we have a district attorney in San Diego willing to right wrongs from the past. Many more innocent inmates are not so lucky, and many will die in prison.

Uriah's story is an important one for everyone to read. It is a story of growth, survival, and hope. It gives a voice to the forgotten men and women behind bars in the country that locks up more of its population than any other on earth. Thanks for telling this story, Uriah.

Professor Justin Brooks
Director, California Innocence Project
California Western School of Law
San Diego, California

Acknowledgments

I really didn't want to undertake this memoir project. I'm not a writer, and I doubted anyone would be interested in my story. I've met many other exonerees who were incarcerated much longer or under far more difficult circumstances than me. You don't have to look far to find someone who has it worse than you do. But people often suggested I write a book, and then Glenda asked about helping me do it.

From the start, my hope has been that God will somehow be glorified through my sharing all these personal details. Revisiting painful places in my mind renewed depression and anxiety, but has also been therapeutic. I've made every effort to be truthful and accurate without hurting other people. The names of a few have been changed to protect their privacy. I pray my story will bless others who have been wrongfully convicted and perhaps provide the impetus for change in a system that—while one of the best in the world—often fails. I want to share how the ability to forgive and rise above bitterness comes only through focusing on Christ.

If not for the Lord working through Glenda, this story would still sit in the dusty bin of my personal history. She took my ramblings and disjointed memories and worked her magic. Given the geographical distance between us and my aversion to technology, this was no easy task. Most anyone else would have thrown up their hands and told me to find another writer. Because she waded with me through the muddy waters of a dark past, she's as much a part of this story now as some people in it.

We wish to express our sincere thanks to all those who walked beside us in this project, especially our families and prayer partners. My brothers and sisters at Christ United Reformed Church supported us in innumerable ways. Kim and Donna Mastalio allowed us to use their home as our office and provided a place for Glenda to stay. Chris and Trisha Olow facilitated her travel to San Diego. These saints and others in far-flung locations repeatedly demonstrated Christ's love to us.

We're grateful for the overwhelming support of the California Innocence Project attorneys and staff, CAPA International Education personnel, as well as exonerees and those involved with the Innocence Movement from around the world. These people realize the importance of this story's call for reform.

When we'd almost given up hope for publication, God brought the Wipf and Stock staff to help us on our way. What a blessing to work with people who allowed us to tell the story freely, yet provided the professional expertise we needed!

Above all, we praise God for equipping us to this work. To him be all the glory forever.

ARREST

Austin, Texas

February 8, 2005

Shouts penetrated my sleep and drug-numbed consciousness.

"US Marshals! Get up!"

Uniformed men rushed into the bedroom, and I bolted upright. Beside me, Jessica shrieked and clutched the blanket to her. Flashlight beams pierced my eyes.

"Uriah Courtney, you're under arrest."

A gun barrel pointed at my head. "Move it, Courtney. You're coming with us."

Rough hands hauled me—naked—from under the covers.

Jessica's arms, pale in the dim room, reached out to me. "Uriah!"

An officer pulled her back. Another held me by an arm, while a third lifted my cargo shorts from the nightstand and handed them to me. With one hand, I struggled into the shorts and fastened them. Then the officer jerked both arms behind my back. Cold handcuffs struck my wrists and clamped shut.

US Marshals and Texas Rangers crowded the room, all with handguns pointed at me. The officer grasping my arms pushed me toward the door. I stumbled down the hall, past a Ranger gripping two-year-old Colton, who squirmed and cried.

I wanted to hug him, but I couldn't even reach out to comfort him with a touch. I gazed into his frightened brown eyes. "Don't worry, buddy." I tried to keep my voice calm. "It'll be all right. Daddy will be back soon."

I thought I spoke the truth. How could I have known I'd be sent to prison for a crime I didn't commit? It would be more than eight years before I'd again hug my son or gaze into his eyes.

3

BEFORE

I

Outdoor Boy

As a five-year-old on the last leg of a flight from Idaho to the US Virgin Islands, I felt like I was embarking on an adventure a million miles from home. I gazed down at the endless blue water, the bluest I'd ever seen. I shivered with anticipation for our arrival because when I'd asked Dad about the weird-looking, canoe-like things on the bottom of the plane, he'd explained they were used for landing in the sea.

As the airplane descended, the blue ocean drew closer. The plane's motor roared, and water splashed against the windows. We magically floated across the surface to a dock. I leapt over the surging water between the bobbing aircraft and the wooden planks. Heat and humidity hit me like an invisible wave, but that strange sensation only increased my rising excitement.

Dad and I stayed in a motel room with a pool right outside the door. What seemed like hundreds of geckos sunned or skittered on the surrounding walls. I spent hours swimming in the warm water and chasing lizards in the brilliant sunshine. Occasionally I'd scoop out the stiff and cold body of a gecko that had fallen into the pool. But warmth radiated through my chest whenever I rescued one that had been swimming around, trying desperately to escape.

One day Dad and I joined a crowd of people on a glass-bottom boat. I pressed my face to the glass and watched colorful fish swim past bright coral reefs. Fish of various sizes and shapes—small or large, round or oval, some with fan tails or spiny fins—all gleaming with colors more vivid and varied than a rainbow. My fingers tingled as I longed to touch them.

The boat slowed and stopped by an island. The captain announced, "If you would like to go swimming or snorkeling, you may do that here."

I grabbed Dad's hand, hopping from one foot to the other, barely able to speak. "Please, Dad, please?"

He laughed and led me to a deckhand, who helped me put on goggles and a life vest. I threw myself into the warm embrace of the ocean. Back and forth I paddled with my face submerged, peering into the sunlit shallows. A school of yellow fish glowed like swimming golden coins. A blue fish sported a neon-green tail. A snake-like eel stirred the sand and a spiny creature crawled on the coral.

I lifted my head and sucked in air.

"Uriah." Dad stood at the railing. "Time to get out."

I plunged my face back under water and continued swimming. Muffled noises filtered to my submerged ears.

Gasping at last for another breath, I again saw Dad. This time leaning over the railing. "Get out of there right now."

The captain's voice came over the speaker. "Time to depart."

I glanced around. I was the only person left in the water. A deckhand stood by the ladder, reaching toward me. I climbed up, dripping with water and excitement.

Every day Dad and I explored our island paradise. I swam or snorkeled in the clear ocean, and we'd walk beside the lapping waves on the beach.

Hermit crabs, digging tiny holes in the sand, fascinated me. When they saw me coming, they'd crawl inside and hide. So I dug my own holes, trying to catch them. I'd hold their shells calmly on my palm until they came out and walked around, carrying their homes on their backs. Curious, I grabbed one by the pincher to see what the rest of it looked like and accidently pulled off its claw. Later one of them pinched me hard enough to pierce my skin, and I thought he was probably paying me back for hurting his friend.

Dad and I found many lovely shells, including one cream-colored scallop. He took his knife from his pocket and bored a small hole in the flat end. Then he threaded a thin strand of leather through the hole, knotted the ends, and slipped it over my head. For years, I wore that shell necklace every day.

*

Our trip to the Virgin Islands would have been perfect, except for one thing—my mother wasn't with us. Even when I chased lizards or splashed in the surging waves, I missed my mom.

I was born in Salmon, Idaho, home to some of the greatest hunting, fishing, and whitewater rafting in the United States. As a small child, I experienced them all. I loved my family and I loved being outdoors. And we enjoyed a whole lot of outdoor activity, especially camping. We often slept in tents and explored remote wilderness areas we called "the sticks." Being outdoors surpassed any toy. Maybe because I was born in small-town Idaho, I've always loved wide-open spaces and blue sky.

In one sense, my childhood was wonderful. But things were not well at home. My parents frequently shouted and argued. I don't remember ever seeing Dad strike Mom, but I once saw the result.

We were camping in a cabin in a wooded area, accessed only by manually pulling a cable car across a river. Dad had put on gloves and grasped the overhead line, hand over hand, heaving the gondola in which we rode across the rushing water. While in that isolated spot, my dad gave my mom a bloody nose.

When I saw the gushing blood, I was very scared, not so much for myself, but for her. I was also angry at him. That memory shaped my attitude as I grew. I detested violence and couldn't fathom how any man could hurt a defenseless woman. When I became an adult, I vowed never to use my hands like that on any woman.

My dad is bipolar and has Post-Traumatic Stress Disorder. As long as I've known him, he's struggled with alcoholism. My mom was my dad's second wife. All in all, Dad has seven children from four marriages. For most of my life, I've had a close relationship with him.

Even when I was very young, Dad took me with him to the Elks Lodge or the Moose Lodge or some other tavern. I loved sitting next to him on a high stool at the bar, drinking my 7Up with a cherry in it, eating a bag of Cheetos, and listening to the amusing adult conversations. I remember peanut shells on the floor of the bar where I first tasted beer.

When I was four, Dad took me to Juneau, Alaska, where he worked on a fishing barge for a few months to make some good and quick money. One day we walked on the massive Mendenhall Glacier, a sheet of aqua ice stretching to the horizon with some peaks high as mountains. We met a man who was soaking wet.

Dad asked, "What happened to you?"

He shivered and wrapped his arms around himself. "I fell through." Then he hurried on.

A short distance farther, we came to an open fissure in the ice. Black water surged below the opening. Dad put his hand on my shoulder and pointed to the gaping hole. "He's lucky he got out. You could fall through and be swept under the ice. Then you'd never find the opening again."

My stomach churned at the thought of being trapped with no hope of escape.

When Dad worked out on the fishing boat, I stayed in a daycare. They made me take naps, and I didn't want to take naps. I missed my dad and wanted to be with him or outside playing.

Not long after Dad and I returned from our Alaskan trip, my parents got divorced. I loved each equally, and their divorce ripped my world apart.

I didn't understand what was going on with my parents' relationship. I felt sad, scared, and confused. Dad decided to help me forget the pain by taking me to the Virgin Islands—an experience that ignited my love for the tropics and fueled my fascination with reptiles. The trip did help me forget about the recent turmoil in my Idaho home, but not about my mom. No matter how much fun I had on that great adventure, I still missed her.

After the divorce, Mom left to live in San Diego. My dad, my brother Taurus, sister Misty, and I moved from Salmon to Coeur d'Alene. When Dad remarried, we moved to a huge house outside Sandpoint, Idaho. A large log rafter ran the length of the house beneath the peak. That place was as country as country gets. The acreage had a barn, sheds, and an orchard to explore. Trains rumbled past on nearby railroad tracks. We lived next to Lake Pend Oreille, Idaho's largest and deepest lake, and skated across its seemingly limitless expanse when it froze over.

After about a year, we moved to a house near the ocean in Waldport, Oregon. Dad and I walked on the beach nearly every day. We collected translucent agates, which we polished in a stone tumbler. We kids made forts by digging big holes in the sand and covering them with driftwood.

After I completed second grade, Taurus, Misty, and I moved to San Diego to live with our mom. While I was reluctant to leave the home by the beach, I looked forward to living with Mom again. I missed her soothing words and soft touch.

But I had no idea how radically different life would be in San Diego.

2

Rebellious Youth

My friend Kelly and I slid down the steep slope, disturbing dirt and dislodging stones—some intentionally—to make small rock slides that tumbled into the ravine below. As the echo of each rumble faded, we glanced at each other and laughed.

Kelly was a couple of years older than me. To my impressionable sixth-grade mind, he seemed strong and smart, and I admired him as if he were an older brother.

We reached the bottom of the wash, dense with trees that blocked the sunlight. But we'd already explored the dim ravine. That had been when we'd discovered the tunnel.

Now we stood before the dark opening that gaped about eight feet wide. Water from the ravine drained into the dark interior, flowing a few inches deep. High on the embankment above, freeway traffic whizzed by. Knowing we were about to walk beneath those whirring motors and whining tires only ratcheted up our excitement.

We sat on a rocky spot near the opening and pulled several plastic grocery bags over our shoes, tying them around our ankles to keep out the water. We were experienced tunnel explorers, our fascination fueled by the popular *Teenage Mutant Ninja Turtles* movie and cartoon show.

Kelly peered into the tunnel. "How far do you s'pose it goes?"

"Who knows?" I joined him at the entrance, my muscles taut with anticipation. "Where do you think it ends up?"

He grinned. "Only one way to find out."

We turned on our flashlights and strode into the tunnel.

It smelled musty. Some tunnels stank, but this one had a pleasant earthy odor. We'd waded into the tunnel only a short distance before my feet felt completely soaked. The water-logged sacks weighed down each shoe.

I stopped. "Some good these bags are."

"Yeah." Kelly bent over and ripped the plastic. "Might as well take them off."

Leaving the torn sacks, we walked on with lighter—if wetter—shoes. Most of the time, we directed the light beams in front of our feet to keep from falling into an unexpected hole. But once in a while, we shone our flashlights down the tunnel. A slight decline allowed us to see farther.

We figured we were about halfway under the freeway when we came to a place with a Y-branch to the right. We stood still. Water dripped from above our heads and gurgled in a current around our ankles.

Even though Kelly couldn't see my face, I smiled. "First stop on our adventure."

He flashed his light back and forth. "Which way?"

"I want to see where both go."

"Let's check out the branch line first."

In no time, we'd reached a large, box-like room with a ceiling so low we'd have to crawl through water. Not wanting to get totally soaked, we headed back to the main line. After we'd been inside the tunnel for almost half an hour, we guessed we were still only a short distance past the freeway. We knew the area well, so we could imagine what was on the surface above our heads.

I shone my light on the concrete ceiling. "You think we're under the street that runs parallel to the freeway?"

"Maybe." Kelly's voice echoed. "Or maybe under one of the apartment buildings next to it."

"How cool would that be, if we were standing right underneath someone's house?"

"Wouldn't it be funny if we made enough noise for them to hear us?"

"Spook the heck out of them, wouldn't it?"

We shrieked and yelled as loudly as we could, between fits of laughter and pauses to catch our breath. When we went on, the tunnel took a very long turn and the descent became steeper. We went around another long, sweeping curve. My sense of thrill and adventure heightened.

But the beam on my flashlight grew dim, and I started to feel uncomfortable. We'd grown a little too confident in our storm drain spelunking abilities and hadn't bothered this time to bring along extra batteries.

My flashlight's feeble beam became barely visible in the dark tunnel. I gulped. "I sure hope this thing comes out somewhere soon."

"We've come a long way." Kelly paused beside me. "Whadda you think? Go back or keep going?"

"I'm not sure exactly where we are."

"Me, either. Those turns mixed up my directions."

I slapped my flashlight against my palm in a vain effort to bring it back to life. "Remember that drain opening full of water we saw a few days ago? It's some place around here. Maybe that's where this tunnel comes out."

"Could be. Might as well go on."

We splashed through the water at a much faster pace. My light died completely, and Kelly's grew dim. We rushed forward with greater urgency for several minutes. Then his light went out.

We stood in utter darkness. It felt heavy. Suffocating.

I took a deep breath, trying to tame the fear that threatened to turn into panic. "Well, we have to be getting close to that opening."

"Sure. Can't be far now." Kelly's trembling voice was my only clue to where he stood.

We shuffled toward each other. Each of us put a hand on the other's shoulder, using our free hands to feel the sides of the tunnel as we moved slowly in the direction we hoped would lead us out.

After what seemed like hours, but was probably only a matter of minutes, we saw a dim light ahead. Relief flooded through me. As soon as the feeble glow illuminated our surroundings, we ran toward the light.

We stopped underneath a rectangular grate and stretched on tiptoe until we could see out. Blue sky gleamed above familiar apartment buildings. We were peering out a storm drain along a street in my neighborhood. Definitely going in the right direction. A renewed thrill surged through me.

The tunnel ran parallel to the street, and at the beginning and end of every block, a grate shed light to guide us.

I said, "This is the coolest tunnel ever."

"No kidding!" Kelly's shout echoed. "We're the tunnel-exploring pros."

Soon we saw daylight streaming through the tunnel's opening. Water surged above our knees as we waded out. We slipped over rocks covered with slimy green algae, and crawdads skittered away from our feet.

We climbed a small embankment, water squishing out our shoes and dripping from our jeans. We blinked in the bright sunshine. Kelly smiled at me.

I grinned back. "I'll never forget today."

*

Exploring storm drains was hardly a safe activity for an elementary school kid, but it was one of the ways I coped with city life in San Diego.

After my large and idyllic country homes in Idaho and Oregon, I struggled to adjust to living in a small apartment in one of America's largest and most densely populated cities. Being surrounded by millions of people, violent gangs, busy freeways, and massive glass buildings towering overhead disoriented me.

When I was younger, I had a mischievous side that was quite harmless and probably not unusual. But when this country boy became a city boy, that ornery aspect increased exponentially. I became a little rebel.

Although the trouble I got into at school was obvious, few people realized the extent of the change. At first, I stole candy and toys from stores. Then my friends and I began stealing bikes or skateboards off porches or balconies. I didn't want to harm others or cause them pain, but I didn't realize stealing something would do that. I sometimes stole things because I wanted them, but mostly for the thrill. Getting away with something illegal or that could get me into trouble was such a rush. The most exciting part was when a security guard at a store or rock quarry or construction site would chase my friends and me. A fast runner, I always got away. In retrospect, I believe that rush may have been an early indicator of an addictive personality. But something was clearly missing in my heart.

The best thing about moving to San Diego was being with my dear mom again. I'm certain she was the one who first told me about God. We only occasionally went to church when I was a kid, but I knew that Mom truly believed in the power of prayer.

She had worked as a secretary at the small hospital in Salmon and got a similar job when she moved to San Diego. Not long after we three siblings arrived to live with her, she began attending nursing school. So she worked, went to school, and raised three kids at the same time.

And we were challenging kids. We fought constantly. In spite of the fighting and arguing, we all loved each other. Mom worked hard to provide for us, and we never lacked basic necessities. We had a home to live in, clothes on our backs, shoes on our feet, and food in our bellies.

Our apartment building stood next to a canyon that quickly became my sanctuary, my little piece of country in the midst of the city. Bike jumps and trails crisscrossed the gorge. In some areas, there was even enough shrubbery to construct a fort. I spent much time down there, riding my bike and catching snakes or lizards. I discovered other nearby canyons, and when I wasn't exploring them, I fished in local ponds or Miramar Lake.

We lived about twenty minutes from the ocean, so I often went to the beach. Boogie boarding and body surfing became favorite water activities.

But when I discovered the vast storm drain system that snaked under the city, I discovered a whole new world. Exploring tunnels both frightened and exhilarated me. I got a thrill from being somewhere forbidden and doing something dangerous, many feet below thousands of people who drove or walked overhead, performing routine daily duties without a clue to my presence. But I also was fascinated by this complex system designed by human ingenuity and constructed with huge machinery.

My friends and I often hid our bikes or skateboards out of sight in the tunnels we explored. Some were narrow and only tall enough to stand upright in, but others were high and wide enough for a construction truck to drive through. We liked large tunnels—the bigger and drier, the better. How enthralling to ride with bike tires humming or skateboard wheels rumbling and our wild shouts echoing off the walls!

A friend and I once pilfered a hundred-count box of road flares from a storage shed. We lit them in a favorite tunnel, illuminating its entire length. Then we zigzagged our bikes around the sputtering flares, hooting and hollering. Back and forth we went, until smoke choked us. As we stumbled through the haze toward the exit, eyes and throats burning, we kicked each flare into the tiny stream of water and watched it fizzle out. Those sputtering flames being snuffed out amused us. A far cry from when the lights went out for Kelly and me.

I now realize how prison sometimes resembled that incident. All light was extinguished, and I was shut off from the world, condemned to dwell in a potentially fatal environment. That darkness was so all-consuming that I felt as if the oxygen were being sucked from my lungs.

But God never left me or forsook me. Just like he caused the sun's rays to shine through narrow drain grates and light the way of escape for two lost souls in a dark tunnel, he provided his Son's light and the Scriptures as a lamp for my path through those perilous years in prison.

It would be a long time, however, before I could see God's hand in my life—and only after a downward spiral that accelerated following a grand theft auto charge at age fourteen.

3

Troubled Teen

My buddies and I came out of the movie theater and scanned the deserted street. It was late, and nothing moved in Mesquite, Nevada.

Jason looked at me. "Looks like we're stuck hitching a ride back."

I shook my head. "Walking back, you mean." We'd tried hitchhiking to Mesquite, but no one had given us a lift so we'd walked the entire twelve miles from Littlefield, Arizona. To rest up, we'd watched the same movie twice. There was no way we could call our parents, who didn't have a clue where we'd gone and would be furious if they found out. We faced a very long walk in the dark.

Brandon set off down the street. "Might as well hit the road."

We shuffled off with far less enthusiasm than when we'd left so many hours earlier. About halfway through town, we walked past the fenced lot of a rental place. Moonlight gleamed on chrome.

I grabbed Brandon's arm. "Hey, look. They have go-karts."

"Dude, we don't even know how to drive those things."

I grinned. "Maybe you don't, but I do."

We snuck along the fence, scurrying from shadow to shadow, until we found the entrance. We broke the padlock on the latch, and the gate creaked open.

"Awesome!" Jason pushed past me.

Brandon dashed inside and glanced around. "Which one's the best?"

One of the karts caught my eye. "I think this one would be the fastest." I smiled. "And fastest is always best."

We pushed it out of the enclosed area to the curb. Main Street was still dead. We looked and listened to make sure no cars were coming. Then we pushed the kart across the street to the parking lot of a Mormon church.

I bent over. "Let's see if we can start this puppy." I flicked on the starter switch and yanked the engine cable. The Briggs and Stratton motor roared to life.

I slipped into the driver's seat. Jason and Brandon straddled the back of the go-kart, each sitting on one side of the frame. They braced their feet behind my seat and grabbed the roll bar above their heads.

Jason whooped. "Take us for a ride, Ry!"

My foot pressed the accelerator, and I eased the kart onto the street.

Brandon tapped my shoulder. "Where you gonna go?"

"Home to Littlefield," I said. "We can hide it in my dad's back shed."

"Are you nuts, Courtney? That's twelve miles from here."

Jason threw back his head and laughed. "Let's do it!"

I floored the pedal and the low-slung kart surged forward, down a quiet side street. Once we got out of town, we took the old highway running parallel to the interstate and soon crossed the Arizona state line. Jason and Brandon were eager to drive, so we took turns, laughing and hollering. The go-kart had no headlights, but the moon was bright enough to guide us. The only way across the river, however, was to get on I-15 and drive over its bridge. Fortunately, no vehicles came up behind us during that brief crossing. We got off the interstate as soon as possible. In Littlefield, I guided the go-kart into our backyard and cut the engine. We pushed it into the shed.

The next morning, Jason and I decided to take it to school. We drove down a little-used dirt road along the top of a bluff beside the Virgin River. We parked the kart in a ravine and covered it with branches. Then we hopped on rocks across the river and walked a quarter mile to school.

Littlefield was a pretty small town, where everyone knew everyone else. Apparently, someone had seen and reported us. During school that day, we were called to the office. A burly sheriff's deputy waited for us with crossed arms. "You boys want to tell me what you did last night?"

*

Stealing the go-kart was a stupid stunt, and driving it across state lines compounded the fallout. All three of us were charged with grand theft auto. I was only fourteen.

Having missed Dad, I'd decided to go back to living with him after I finished seventh grade. During eighth grade in Littlefield, I transformed from a rebellious child to a deeply troubled teenager.

At the time, Littlefield was simply a string of houses and trailer homes scattered along the desert valley. Although it was hot and desolate, I liked the place. A short walk from our house led me to the Virgin River, where I swam and explored the river bottom. I often took a dip in a nearby freshwater spring.

But outdoor exploration and play no longer satisfied my desire for thrills. I began smoking pot at thirteen. When I was fourteen, my dad and I started smoking pot and drinking together.

I occasionally stole something or damaged property, but now I was way more interested in drinking booze, getting high, and chasing girls. I never felt good enough for anyone or anything, and that seemed to justify messing around with easy girls. I had always been shy, so when I discovered how drugs and alcohol lowered my inhibitions, I ran with it. I seldom left home without getting loaded, and if I did, it was to get loaded. I can truthfully say that from age fourteen on, with few exceptions, I didn't stay a day sober.

Drugs and alcohol were my bosom buddies, my favorite companions. I took pride in being able to party harder than any of my friends. I had a reputation to live up to, and I literally almost died trying.

My brush with death happened during the brief time we lived in Hurricane, Utah, only long enough for me to complete ninth grade. My friends and I had a favorite partying spot behind my house. No one could see us sitting on the slanted concrete slab beneath a bridge spanning a wash.

One night I drank an entire fifth of Crown Royal whiskey within about fifteen minutes, and then I smoked pot on top of it. My mind blanked out after that. My stepbrother, Anthony, told me later that I began shouting and acting crazy. I walked onto the bridge and yelled up at the sky.

The cops soon arrived. Assuming I was on a hallucinogenic drug, they called for an ambulance. My dad and stepmom heard sirens and walked down to the bridge, where they discovered I was the source of the commotion.

At the hospital, emergency room personnel had to strap me down and cut off my clothes in order to treat me. They pumped my stomach and put me on an IV drip. Evidently they also attempted to absorb the toxins in my system by forcing me to ingest activated charcoal, because I vomited the black stuff all over the white linoleum. A pretty young nurse had to clean it up, and I was so embarrassed that I kept apologizing to her.

A doctor came in and leaned over me. "You're lucky to be alive, young man."

I still grieve to remember Dad sitting at my bedside and crying. "What are you doing to yourself, Uriah? Do you want to be just like me?"

A few days after my alcohol poisoning incident, the husband of a kind teacher contacted me. A Native American medicine man, he asked me to accompany him to a ceremony at nearby sacred Indian grounds. Being a lover of Indian culture, I went. Dad came along.

The ceremony took place mid-morning on a beautiful sunny day, high in the mountains with a panoramic view of Hurricane Valley and St. George, Utah. A brilliant blue sky stretched over the meadow, dotted with scrub oak and fragrant with pinion pines and cedar trees. We sat around a small fire, passing and smoking an Indian peace pipe. The medicine man told us the pipe had been handed down from generation to generation and was 400 years old. The bowl was cut from stone, the stem carved from cherry wood. Hawk and eagle feathers hung from leather thongs—narrow as string—wrapped around the stem. The "tobacco" was a nonintoxicating tribal blend of natural herbs and plants. After we finished passing the peace pipe, the medicine man sang and chanted while Dad and I beat deer-hide drums.

My Native American friend believed my erratic behavior was caused by bad spirits, and his purpose was to drive them from me. I didn't buy that, but I appreciated his efforts and found the ceremony fascinating. I still admire how Native Americans respect and cherish the earth for its beauty. That day I was seeking a mystical experience. Now I realize that it linked my love for nature with a deep spiritual longing. But my behavior didn't change.

The following year, my family moved to a scenic eighty-acre property fifteen miles from Kanab, Utah. Our nearest neighbor was three miles away. While we built our house, Dad, my stepbrother, and I lived in a tent at first and then in a small travel trailer during the winter.

We camped, fished, and hiked regularly—truly roughing it. Although it was kind of tough for a teenager to live so far from friends, I loved the area's rugged beauty. Sunlight and cloud shadows played on the face of a nearby mountain range that glowed with pink, orange, and tan sandstone.

When I was sixteen and seventeen, I enjoyed two tropical vacations, one with my mom and one with my dad. The trip with Mom consisted of driving three days from San Diego all the way down to Cabo San Lucas, Baja Mexico, where we tented for twelve days on the beach. My stepbrother and I snorkeled in the shallow water or fished with Hawaiian sling spears that were nine feet long. Once I dove down to a rocky outcropping on the sea floor. I stuck my head in a hole and held still until my eyesight adjusted to the gloom. Then I found myself staring into the beady eyes of an eel.

The trip with Dad was reveling for two weeks in the tropical paradise of Costa Rica. And for me, it was paradise. Good food, strong drink, beautiful women, and abundant drugs—the only things I cared about. I didn't want to return to the States, not only because of my completely debauched lifestyle, but because I loved the clean and captivating warm ocean, the deep green and dense jungle, all the beautiful birds, animals, and reptiles (including crocodiles), and the friendly people.

But I returned to Kanab with my family. By this time, Dad and I were drinking and using drugs together occasionally. We were like best friends, and I enjoyed getting high with him. He didn't introduce me to drugs; I was already using them on my own. But when he found out what I was up to, we started partying together. Obviously, this was a wreck waiting to happen. I won't deny it, we had some crazy fun times together, but we also had many fights, verbal and physical. One time, he punched me in the face.

Around the middle of eleventh grade, I wanted to drop out of high school. I was a full-blown alcoholic, pothead, and frequent user of harder drugs. School bored me, and I was just plain tired of going. The only thing that mattered to me was getting loaded.

Due to my behavioral problems and a diagnosis of Attention Deficit Disorder, I was in special education classes off and on throughout high school. My special ed teacher, Stan Serafin, knew I was ready to give up. He encouraged me to get the credits I needed in order to graduate.

"Listen, Uriah," he said, "if you take only required classes for the rest of eleventh grade and the first trimester of twelfth, you can finish school early."

Early sounded good to me. "Yeah?"

"Yes. Then you can come back later to graduate with your fellow seniors."

He worked with me to bring my grades up to As and Bs. I also stopped getting into trouble, but not partying. At the end of the first trimester in my senior year, I was given the option of staying in school or leaving. I left.

Mr. Serafin was a great teacher. He was patient, kind, and passionate about teaching. If it hadn't been for his help, I wouldn't have graduated. He knew I had problems, but he saw the occasional beam of potential gleam through, and he wanted to help make it shine even brighter.

He and I often conversed about life. A recovering alcoholic and drug user with over thirty years' sobriety, he understood my struggles. He was the best teacher I ever had and the only one who seemed to truly care.

Regrettably, I failed to follow his advice to participate in my senior class graduation ceremony. However, I did go back to Kanab a year later to pick up my diploma. A very sweet school secretary had kept it in her desk drawer all that time. She knew me well from having seen me in the principal's office so often. Proud of me for graduating, she even announced over the intercom that I had come in to get my diploma.

Because I was fast and athletic, football and wrestling coaches tried recruiting me throughout high school, but I refused. Getting high was more important to me. So many lost opportunities. And more would follow.

This time frame marked a turning point in my spiritual life. When I was a child, I prayed to God before I went to bed each night, asking him for things. As my addictions grew worse in my teen years, I prayed less and less. One day I actually spit in God's face.

I wandered in the wilderness somewhere near our Kanab property, stumbling around in the woods, stoned on pot and alone—except for a very large bottle of cheap wine.

I rambled aimlessly, mumbling to myself. "I hate life. I hate myself."

Tripping on a rock, I fell to one knee and almost dropped my bottle. I wobbled to my feet and looked at the sky. "I hate God."

Nothing happened. I stumbled on until I came to the edge of a plateau and ambled around its rocky rim. I looked down at the gold-colored grass waving in the breeze. The prairie stretched for miles, and I could see across the state line into Arizona. Even in my messed-up mental state, I was so struck by the incredible beauty of the scene that it remains vivid in my mind.

For years afterward, I wondered how I could have been so miserable and still awed by beauty. Much later, when I learned about how God created the world and still shows himself through nature, I suddenly understood that God had been revealing himself to me all along. My heart had just been too hard and my ears too deaf to hear his voice.

In my distress that day, I flung myself down, peering over the precipice at the sheer cliff face and prairie far below. It was as if I could see the shape of every rock and every blade of grass in sharp relief. As I stared in wonder at the external beauty, my internal ugliness overpowered me.

"I want to die." I gazed at the ground far below. "Why not just step off? Put an end to all my misery?"

I began to cry. "Why did you even bring me into this world, God?" I rolled over and shook my fist at the sky. "I hate you! I want you out of my life!"

Eventually I lurched back home and passed out. I didn't think life could get any worse. But I would soon plummet into a darker abyss than I'd ever imagined.

4

Wild Adult

Marijuana smoke filled my tiny apartment. I half-reclined on the fold-out couch, drinking vodka and smoking a joint with Big Daddy, a Mexican gang member who'd been in and out of prison for violent crimes.

He started arguing with me over nothing. Without warning, he lunged forward and grabbed me by the throat. Then he punched me in the face, so hard the blow flung me against the back of the couch.

He threw himself on top of me, pulled a knife from his pants, and held it to my throat. He began cursing and crying. "I'm gonna kill you, Ariah."

The man reeked of alcohol, and his stench made me want to retch. The cold blade pressed against my neck. Tears filled his dilated eyes.

With his 300 pounds crushing me and his massive, tatted arms pinning mine down, I was helpless. I tried to swallow my fear. "Calm down, man. Everything's cool."

Tears poured down his brown cheeks and snot dripped from his nose. His uncontrolled sobbing terrified me. He was obviously out of his mind. I had no doubt he would slit my throat.

He swore, calling me every name in his extensive cursing vocabulary. He repeated over and over, "I'm gonna kill you, Ariah."

"You don't want to do it, Big Daddy," I gasped for air to keep speaking. "Please. Please, stop this. It's all cool."

"I gonna kill you, Ariah, you sonofabitch."

He sobbed and pressed the knife's sharp edge into my skin. I took what I thought was my last breath. "Don't do it," I begged.

Finally, he stopped crying, got up, and walked out. The door to his apartment across the outside walkway slammed shut.

Lying limply in the same position he'd left me, I stared at the ceiling. My mind reeled. I could hardly believe I still lived. I tentatively touched my throat and glanced at my fingertips, expecting to see blood. I'd been drinking and getting high all day, but that incident sobered me right up. It shook me so badly, I immediately got loaded again.

For the next few weeks, the memory of that attack grew like a cancer in my brain. Every day, I'd see Big Daddy coming and going across the walkway. I'd stew on what he'd done and what could have happened. Until one day I went crazy.

Drunk and high, I punched out all the windows of my studio apartment with my bare hands. Blood flowing from my hands and arms, I ran in bare feet—wearing only a pair of shorts—down the walkway and into the street. I dashed around, yelling and stumbling against cars, streaking windshields and hoods with bright red blood.

When the cops showed up, I ran back to barricade myself in my studio with my stepbrother, Anthony. The police pounded on the door and shot mace through the broken windows. Anthony hunkered on the floor until he couldn't take the mace any longer. Then he crawled to the door and opened it for the cops. I resisted arrest so wildly they thought I was hallucinating. Eventually they subdued me and transported me to a county mental health facility. The staff there drugged me and let me sleep it off.

The next day, I went back to my studio and replaced every window.

*

Big Daddy's attack may have triggered the window-smashing incident, but that was only the first in a series of self-destructive episodes. I had little sense of personal worth and a low view of life. Certainly my drug use and alcohol abuse messed up my mind. Whatever the reasons behind my actions, my life as a young adult was a split-personality mix of responsible employment juxtaposed with out-of-control behavior.

After I'd completed my high school requirements and a trip to Florida, I realized how much my relationship with my dad had deteriorated. I soon returned to San Diego. My mom's boyfriend, Rick Gambino, had offered to help me get into construction.

Rick got me hired on as his apprentice and gave me a great start in the building trade, especially in metal stud framing and hanging sheetrock.

Soon after I moved into my small apartment, I drove to Utah and brought Anthony back to share the studio and work with me.

But my window-breaking stunt got us evicted. We worked out of town for a while, and eventually moved in with my dad, who now lived in Pahrump, Nevada. There's basically nothing but desert for miles around; it's hot, windy, and dusty. Most people would consider it ugly and barren, but I liked the wide-open spaces and the huge, blue sky. At night, you could see millions of stars—often shooting stars streaking across the black expanse.

Dad had a pit bull that took to me. I called him Kid Dog, and we were inseparable. If I'd sing or holler, he'd throw back his head and howl. It was so hilarious that I'd howl, too, and we'd sit with our heads together, howling like a couple of coyotes.

I took Kid Dog everywhere with me. He would ride in the back of the pickup, even when I went out partying. By now, I was hooked on harder drugs, plus my drinking was completely unchecked. It wasn't long before madness overtook me again, this time with disastrous consequences.

On my way home from partying one night, I blew a tire and continued driving. The metal rim on the rough, washboard road made a terrible racket, and Dad heard me coming from a mile away. When I drove on the yard, he strode out of the house, shouting and swearing. He swung at me and connected.

Something snapped inside me. I wasn't about to take this from him—the man who'd hit my mom and had once punched me in the face. Rage overwhelmed me, and I hit him. Again. And again. I was angry and wanted to punish him, but—even in my inebriated state—I didn't want to kill him.

This part of my past haunts me to this day. Later I apologized to Dad. I've confessed this sin to the Lord and I know that I'm forgiven, but thinking about how badly I beat up my own father still fills me with shame.

The cops arrived and arrested me with much force because I resisted them—even kicking out the patrol car window barefooted. They sprayed my face with mace and put a bag over my head so I couldn't spit on them. At the jail, they fastened me into a restraining chair. I struggled against the straps, my maced eyes burning and confused mind churning.

Where was Kid Dog? He'd been in the back of the pickup on my way home. What had happened to him? Worried about my dog, I yelled for him. Then I threw back my head and howled.

When I sobered up after a few hours and was put in general population, the inmates laughed and teased me about howling so loudly they'd heard me from their cells.

Unlike my relationship with my father, Kid Dog had survived with no harm. But that foray into insanity earned me DUI charges (driving under the influence), as well as charges for resisting arrest, minor consumption, and domestic battery. It also initiated my felony record at age nineteen.

I can't even say how often I went wild and was subsequently arrested. The charges were always alcohol related. Somehow the arresting officers never discovered drugs.

One day, while I waited to appear in court, a sheriff's deputy sat down and talked to me. "You know, Uriah, you're a really nice guy. But you wouldn't believe how crazy you get when you're drunk. I wish I could show you a video of the things you do then."

For about three years, I lived in a half dozen different places in Pahrump. My dad, stepmom, and younger sister had moved to Arizona, and Anthony moved there later, so I had no family around. A couple of times, I slept in the back of my truck with Kid Dog until I found a new place to live.

Unfortunately, Kid Dog died while I was at work one day. I cried like a baby when I found him dead. I loved that dog.

Despite my party life, I managed to hold down a regular job from the beginning of my stay in Pahrump. I worked on a new tract housing project and quickly picked up on wood framing, developing a good reputation as a hard worker, fast and dependable. I enjoyed construction and worked with a number of carpenters I considered like brothers, even though some were old enough to be my father.

One became a drinking buddy after hours, and I got to know his family. He had a beautiful wife, but he cheated on her and abused her. Because I actually did things with their son, I became a father figure to him. I attended his sports games, took him bowling, and went hiking with him.

Although this woman was eleven years older than I was, we developed a sexual relationship. Jessica became pregnant while she was still married, so I didn't know if I was the father. One day she'd tell me the baby was mine, and the next she'd say he wasn't. This greatly distressed me, and the drugs and alcohol exacerbated my anguish.

The day I found out Jessica was giving birth in Las Vegas and hadn't let me know, I went nuts. I ended up getting arrested for evading police in a vehicle, DUI, damage to public property, bribing an officer of the law (although that had not been my intent), and damage to a police vehicle. When I came to my senses, I was stricken with remorse for what I'd done. Years later, after I'd been proved innocent of the charges for which I was wrongfully convicted, this arrest in Nevada would come back to torment me.

In an effort to escape my problems, I decided to return to southern California. I thought I was leaving my troubles behind, but all my personal issues accompanied me. And they would come to a head in San Diego.

5

Broken Man

My mind foggy from drugs, I drove my 1995 Ford Thunderbird away from my friend's house. As soon as I turned the first corner, red and blue lights flashed in my rearview mirror.

I swore and pulled over. No time to stash my drug kit. I stuck a bag of meth between the passenger seat and console. Some pills were in the glove compartment. But at least the only drugs in large enough amounts to exceed the personal-use measure were just a couple of ounce bags of skunkbud (pungent pot).

The policeman came up to my car, and I rolled down the window.

"Anything wrong, officer?"

"Whew!" He raised his eyebrows. "Smells like you've got some strong pot in there. Why don't you step out of the car so I can have a look?"

"Why'd you stop me?"

"I pulled you over because you didn't have your headlights on." He peered inside the car. "May I see your license?"

I opened my wallet and took out my license. He looked at it. "Step out of the vehicle, Mr. Courtney."

I opened the door and slowly got out.

He motioned for me to turn around. "Up against the car. Spread your feet. Put your hands behind your head and interlock your fingers."

I complied.

That moment remains extremely vivid. I gazed at the twinkling lights of the distant shipyards. Shining from the tops of cranes jutting into the sky and from the decks of ships in the docks, the glittering lights and their rippling reflections seemed mocking. A feeling of loss pierced me as I wondered how long it might be before I saw those lights again.

I'd moved back to San Diego in 2003, a wounded and broken man, full of trouble with the law and in my soul. I was on probation in Nevada for multiple alcohol-related incidents, but I was permitted to go to San Diego on an interstate compact. The conditions were that I stay sober, go to Alcoholics Anonymous (AA), and do community service.

I didn't stay sober. I maintained only a pretense of going to AA and doing community service. My life became even more depraved. Truly, I was a friend of the devil and didn't know it.

In San Diego, I worked again for my stepdad. He had obtained his contractor's license and had developed a good professional reputation. That was a terrific job. I was paid prevailing wages and traveled all over San Diego County, performing various aspects of commercial construction work on post offices, but rarely doing the same thing twice.

Initially I lived with my brother, Taurus, his wife, and four kids. I loved being around family again. Taurus and I often enjoyed doing things together, including drinking. But alcohol now was mostly a thing of the past. For me, it was all about meth.

Meth steals your appetite and your sleep. I enjoyed not only the high from speed, but also the weird euphoric feeling I'd get from being awake for days. When I discovered that food helped me stay awake longer, I forced myself to eat regularly. Most addicts suffer from hallucinations when they go more than two or three days without sleep, but I didn't. I liked to be awake and high ("tweaking") as long as possible. I could be up for a week or more with no problem.

I sometimes made weekend trips to Pahrump, leaving after work on Friday and not sleeping until after work on Monday. I went there to party with old friends and visit Jessica. I'd see her baby, Colton, but refused to believe he was my son. Still, I had a special affection for him. But then she and her sons moved to Texas.

When Taurus discovered I was a meth addict, he made me leave. I moved in with my sister Misty, her husband Kyng, and their three kids. Misty and Kyng knew about my addiction and were concerned about me, but let me live in their garage that had been converted into a playroom and entertainment area.

Early one morning, I was up tweaking as usual when Kyng came in before he left for work. He talked to me about what I was doing with my life.

He pulled a little Bible from his pocket and read something from the Psalms. I don't remember what he read, but I was touched by his compassion.

Kyng was a good man and a great father. He believed in Christ and truly loved my sister. He was patient, kind, and always wore a smile. Whenever he spoke to me about God and the Bible, I'd pretend interest for the moment and then go off and forget about it.

After a few months, I began living with a woman—a fellow druggie—in an area of San Diego many people would consider ghetto. She had congestive heart failure, and her doctor told me that continued drug use would kill her. Not wanting such a thing on my conscience, I took her to live with her ex-husband, with whom she still had an amicable relationship.

My troubles with the law continued in San Diego. I worked during the day, but when I was spun out on meth I was awake for long periods of time. I often spent those nights retrieving metals to recycle, and I'm ashamed to admit that sometimes I stole them. I was cited once for petty theft, and then I was arrested for stealing copper cable from a section of trolley tracks under construction. I was charged with felony vandalism and grand theft. It would have been much worse had I not stashed my drug kit in the bushes before I picked up the cable. I was taken to county jail and made bail a couple hours later. When I got out, I reclaimed my truck from impound and returned to the arrest site to pick up my dope kit.

Getting arrested for anything was a probation violation, and if Nevada discovered this, I would be extradited to serve a year in jail. So I hired an attorney to deal with the matter. For the time being, Nevada hadn't found out about it. If they had, I would have been in jail there and never accused of what would soon happen.

I didn't need to steal, but sometimes temptation lay in front of me as tangibly as that cable. Stealing fed my desire for thrills. And my rebellious nature led me to hate the law. I thought they (whoever "they" might be) owed me something for all the wrongs I felt I had suffered and for previous fines I had paid. I now see how skewed my thinking was in those days.

The arrest when I was pulled over after leaving my friend's house would prove more serious than any previous ones. I knew at the time I was in deep trouble, but it turned out far worse than I'd anticipated.

Of course, the cops discovered the drugs and dope kit in my car as well as a large quantity of cash in my back pocket. These things no doubt screamed "drug dealer" to them. But that wasn't the case, and I had nothing indicating sales with me except the two bags of pot.

Yet behind my seat, they claimed to have found a paper bag full of rock cocaine in multiple baggies. I say "claimed" because it wasn't mine and I didn't put it there. I used rock cocaine, but never sold it and didn't have any on me then. They apparently planted it to secure an arrest for transportation for sale, because—except for the pot—none of my drugs were bagged up or prepared for selling. This might sound unbelievable, considering all the other stuff they found, but it's the truth.

I was charged with eleven felony counts related to transportation for sales and violations of health and human safety codes. I was booked downtown, and sent to George Bailey Detention Facility.

While there, I attended chapel service and enjoyed hearing the Bible read and discussed. After about ten days in jail, I had some kind of emotional experience. I prayed and swore to God that I would continue praying, if he would get me out of the mess I'd gotten myself into.

Sadly, the experience had little effect on me. A day or two later, I made bail. I met the bondsman at the bar of a restaurant and got drunk with him. I left the restaurant and went right back to getting high.

I did, however, feel compelled to better care for the much-older woman with whom I was living and her six-year-old son. About a week after I got out of jail, I rented a nice little house for us. Her son was a good kid, and I was quite fond of him. We enjoyed doing things together, and I wanted to provide this woman and boy with a roof over their heads.

One day I told her I'd promised God to start praying again if I got out of jail, and I confessed how the failure to keep my promise made me feel extremely convicted night and day. She told me I had better start praying then. I didn't, and over time I just forgot about it in the fog of addiction.

During the subsequent months after I'd posted bail, I had a few court hearings, including one at which a letter from my stepdad testified that I would be working for him under his supervision. Rick was fed up with my behavior at that point, but under pressure from my family, he agreed to write the note.

Because I also hired an attorney and made a plea bargain, my case didn't go as badly as it might have. At the final hearing in October of 2004, I was sentenced to three months in work furlough and three years probation. I was given one month to get my things in order. I made sure my friend had enough money for rent, utilities, and groceries. But personally, I grew even worse. The stress of facing confinement—caged away from the blue sky and fresh air, isolated from my family and friends—led me to dive even deeper into drugs.

I checked into work furlough a few days after Thanksgiving. Rick picked me up on work mornings and took me to our current jobsite. I still used a little meth every day, despite knowing this was a probation violation and that I could be drug-tested at any time.

On December 19, while checking in after work, I tested positive for meth. I was told to go to my room, grab my belongings, and get ready to be transported to county jail.

Accompanied by a staff person, I went to the room I shared with three others and packed a duffle. As we entered the courtyard—without giving it any thought—I dropped my bag, jumped a fence that surrounded the facility, and pelted down the street. I had no plan. I simply couldn't face incarceration and took the opportunity to make a break for it.

After running a while, I hid under a parked car and then a bridge about a mile away. From there, I called my friend and told her what had happened and asked her to pick me up. She did.

Knowing a warrant would be issued for my escape, I couldn't stay at my house. I lived in a motel until I found a drug rehab that would take me in. Someone from the rehab told me about an attorney who could help me, and I hired him. I was told that if I remained in rehab for a time and then turned myself in, it would go better for me in court. That became my plan.

While in rehab, I had a DNA test to determine if I was really Colton's father and waited for the results. I also had random drug tests. The first time I tested positive for meth, I received a warning. The second time—only about a month after I'd arrived—I was kicked out of the program. My grand plan evaporated.

Again I had my friend pick me up and take me to a motel. I bounced around for a few days, trying to figure out how to salvage the situation. I intended to turn myself in, but I wanted to make an effort at reconciliation with Jessica first. I felt I could face the inevitable prison time if I could anticipate our future together. Hoping for the best, I took a beautiful engagement ring with me to Texas.

Jessica picked me up at the airport. Early the next morning, I prepared to go for a walk.

Two-year-old Colton saw me tying my shoe laces. "Where you goin'?"

"I'm going to take a walk. I won't go far."

He extended his arms for me to pick him up. Because I'd just arrived and was basically a stranger to him, Jessica and her mother were astonished. I scooped him up, and he immediately rested his head on my shoulder.

As I walked around the cul-de-sac with him in my arms, I experienced a wide range of new and strange feelings. Mostly joy. At this point, I didn't even know Colton was my son and I didn't care. This precious little boy clung to me, and it was the most heartwarming thing I'd ever experienced. I wanted to believe he was my son, but whether he was or not, I longed to be a part of his life. Jessica was now free from her ex-husband, and I decided that if she would have me I would marry her and raise both boys—her older son and the little guy in my arms. They were children in need of a father, and I hoped to be just that. That meaningful moment affected me profoundly.

The next afternoon, I accessed the DNA testing company's website and viewed my results. I was, indeed, Colton's biological father. I picked him up and carried him to his mom's room, where I hugged them both and shed tears of joy. I cannot describe the plethora of my thoughts and emotions. After denying it in my mind for two years, the reality of holding my own son in my arms jolted through me like an electric current.

There was no question that I was going to be a part of my son's life from then on. I asked Jessica to marry me and gave her the ring.

Eight days after I arrived at her home, US Marshals—assisted by Texas Rangers—arrested me at gunpoint.

At the time, I wasn't terribly surprised at the arrest because of my escape from work furlough in San Diego. But the number of officers and the amount of force they used did seem a little overboard.

The image of my son, crying hysterically in one officer's arms as another led me past in handcuffs, still pains me. I told Colton that everything would be all right. I expected to go away for no more than a year.

It would be weeks before I'd discover what I actually faced. And first, I'd have to live my personal nightmare—confinement in a very dark place.

AFTER

6

True Unknown

Travis County Jail

On the other side of the visiting window, Jessica held the phone receiver away from her ear and sobbed into her other hand. I wanted so badly to reach through the thick glass, cradle her in my arms, and tell her that everything would be all right. But I couldn't touch her. Due to my status as a high-level inmate, I was permitted only an occasional no-contact visit. This meant seeing Jessica through a blurry glass barrier and hearing her through a scratchy, distant-sounding telephone connection.

I touched the dirty glass, smeared with fingerprints. "Please don't cry, babe." If she kept it up, I was sure to dissolve into tears, too.

She sniffed and pressed the phone against her ear again. "What are we going to do, Uriah?"

"Don't worry. Once I pay my dues, we'll go on with our wedding plans."

She wiped her eyes with a crumpled tissue. "But how long will that be?"

"Maybe a year or so, not long."

Her tears flowed again. "It seems so unfair! We'd just gotten back together after being apart for a year. I don't want to wait another entire year."

I squeezed my hand into a fist on the filthy counter. "I don't want to wait either, but somehow we'll get through this."

Jessica lowered her voice. "Uriah, I have to tell you something."

I leaned forward. "What is it, babe?"

"I think I'm pregnant."

I caught my breath as elation surged through me. "Pregnant? We were only together for about a week. Are you sure?"

She nodded. "Pretty sure. I'm never this late. And I've been feeling sick in the mornings."

My newly discovered sense of fatherhood soared. After all the uncertainty and distress with not knowing whether or not Colton was my son, this was the real deal. There was no doubt this child was mine. The thought of my baby growing inside her womb thrilled me.

"That's terrific, Jessica." I placed my palm on the glass and smiled. "How exciting! We'll be a real family."

She shook her head. "I don't know, Uriah. How can I go through pregnancy and childbirth without you? How can I raise a baby and two boys by myself?"

My eyes locked onto hers. "It won't be long. I promise."

She raised her eyebrows.

"I mean it," I assured her. "I'll do my time, and when I get out, I'll find a job and provide a home for us."

Her watery eyes widened. "I'm scared, Uriah."

"So am I." I swallowed the panic in my throat. "But somehow we'll get through this. Together."

*

Jessica's visits are among my clearest memories from the confused time in Travis County Jail in Texas. Just when I finally anticipated a future with a family of my own, the arrest had ripped me from the people I loved. Because I faced an unknown future that would certainly include a year or so in prison, my emotional state was volatile.

The US Marshals had told me only that I was wanted on a warrant from San Diego. I was told nothing else. Because I assumed I was being arrested for fleeing from work furlough, I didn't even ask for any more information.

A day or two after I entered the jail, I found a Bible and started reading it. I was not a reader and had no inclination to read anything, let alone something so archaic and foreign. But I read the Bible, beginning at the first page. That's how you read a book, right? I was drawn to that Bible like a bee to a bright flower brimming with nectar.

This new experience calmed my chaotic mind. Describing its spiritual effect eludes me. At the time, I didn't consider it significant—although I remember being quite taken with the Psalms and Proverbs.

I remained in jail in Texas a little over two weeks, rarely leaving my cell—even when the dayroom was open—except to take a shower or make a phone call. Most of the time, I'd sit or lie on my bed and read the Bible.

Within days, my simple interest blossomed into a hunger. I devoured Scripture. But I didn't intend to genuinely change. Instead, I pondered on my bed how I was going to be a smarter, better, and more responsible drug addict. After I served a little time in county jail, I'd move my new family to San Diego and be a better man for them. But I was not willing or able to give up meth. Speed was my first love; everyone else came second. I actually believed I was going to have it all: a beautiful wife, children, a nice house, a good job, and—of course—meth.

As I sat in the Texas jail, building castles in the air, I didn't realize what was happening back in San Diego.

During the few days I'd stayed with Jessica, I'd received a call from someone at my storage facility, telling me there had been a fire and I needed to come and give them a list of my belongings with their estimated value. Of course, I didn't fall for it. I figured it was a ruse to get me to visit my storage unit in the hope of arresting me.

What I wouldn't find out for a long while was that someone had tipped off police about the unit and it had already been searched. Law enforcement officials had discovered some guns, drug paraphernalia, and cash. It looked like they'd caught a big fish (although things were not as they appeared). Authorities fabricated a story that I had pried open a door to escape work furlough. I was placed second from the top on San Diego's most wanted list and was considered armed and dangerous.

Many different law enforcement agencies came to Mom and Rick's house at all hours of the night and day, multiple times, looking for me. Rick was furious with me for running from work furlough, getting them dragged into a fugitive search, and causing my mom such worry and heartache.

Learning all this after the fact, it's no longer a surprise why the Marshals and Rangers used such force when they arrested me. Were they aware that California was interested in me for the accusations still to come? I don't know.

When I appeared at an extradition hearing while in Texas, the only thing brought up was that I had a warrant in California. I didn't fight the extradition. In fact, I asked to be sent back immediately. I accepted full responsibility for my actions and was willing to pay the price.

On February 23, 2005, a deputy woke me early in the morning and told me to get ready to be extradited. I gathered my few belongings and sat on my bunk, waiting for them to open the cell door.

A short time later, I was taken to ground level where two US Marshals waited.

"Uriah Courtney?"

I nodded. "Yes. That's me."

"You're being extradited to California, and we'll be escorting you to San Diego."

The other Marshal leveled his gaze at me. "You going to give us any trouble?"

"Of course not."

They gave me a gray hoodie with a pocket in the front. I stuck one hand through and out the other side. They put handcuffs on me and I pulled my shackled wrists inside the pocket.

They drove me to the airport in Austin, and we flew to Los Angeles, and then on to San Diego in a smaller plane. Then they transported me in a federal vehicle to San Diego Central Jail, located in the downtown area.

As we drove past businesses, I asked, "Would you guys stop at a taco shop and get me a burrito, since it will be my last one for the next year or so?"

They replied together, "No."

I don't know if they had any idea how wrong I was about the length of my incarceration. I only know I was clueless about what I'd learn in San Diego.

7

Shocking Revelation

San Diego Central Jail

An intercom announcement from the control booth blared in my cell. "Uriah Courtney, get up and prepare for court."

With a pounding heart, I jumped off my rack (the cell shelf that passes for a bed). I unfolded the single thin blanket I used for a pillow. No need to get dressed. It was cold enough I slept in every item of issued clothing: one pair of underwear, socks, white T-shirt, and blue polyester pants and shirt.

At the door of the module, a sheriff's deputy greeted me with a set of shackles. One chain snaked around my waist with handcuffs attached on short chains over each hip. The deputies herded the shackled inmates onto an elevator, and we rode from the seventh floor down to the second. There we waited in filthy and crowded holding tanks, kept icy cold to discourage the growth of germs.

After I'd shivered from the temperature and dread for a couple hours, deputies escorted me across the street to the massive old San Diego County Courthouse. They put me inside another holding cell. Some time later, my name was called and I was led into a courtroom where a blind judge presided over the bench.

My mom sat in the courtroom and smiled when I caught sight of her.

As the hearing began, I stood next to a tall, court-appointed attorney.

The judge listed the charges. "Uriah Courtney, you are charged with kidnapping, rape by foreign object, assault with intent to commit sexual penetration, false imprisonment, and robbery."

He continued with more legal jargon, but I couldn't process any additional words. Kidnapping? Rape? Robbery? My heart felt like a cold stone and my whole body wavered. Barely able to stand, I stared at the judge with my mouth hanging open, stunned beyond belief.

He spoke about a sixteen-year-old female. I turned to my attorney. "What in the heck is going on?"

"Shush." He fixed his eyes on the judge.

I tried to focus my disoriented mind as the judge talked about an assault that took place on November 24, 2004. I shook my head. "That's not me." I raised my trembling voice. "You have the wrong man."

My attorney hushed me again.

The district attorney spoke. "Your honor, I ask that Uriah Courtney be denied bail because he is a flight risk. He has an outstanding escape charge against him, having previously fled from work furlough."

The judge denied the request for no bail, but set it so high I had no hope of making it.

Waves of terror and disbelief rolled through me. I recall very little of what was actually said, but I vividly remember my panic and confusion. These were serious charges, and I knew they'd carry significantly longer sentences than I'd expected. I'd suddenly gone from looking at a year to far more years, possibly even the rest of my life. My mind and body seemed to shut down, and I felt completely numb.

Afterward, I looked at my attorney. "What's this all about? Where did these charges come from?"

He shook his head. "I'm not sure, Uriah. I don't know what's going on myself." He patted my shoulder. "I'll look into it and get back to you."

I have no memory of being returned to my cell. I only recall sitting on my bunk, staring into space in a state of total bewilderment and fear. Before me, I saw nothing but eternal blackness and isolation. I wanted the pain and terror to end. I just wanted to die.

*

Mom was able to set up an appointment to visit me that same day (March 5, 2005). Years later, she told me how she, too, had gone into a state of shock upon hearing the horrible charges. But that evening, she did her best to encourage me.

"Be strong, Uriah." Tears flowed down her cheeks unchecked. "I need you to be strong for me."

Her obvious grief pierced my heart. I couldn't stand to see her tears and I dropped my head.

Mom tapped the glass between us and spoke louder into the phone. "Listen to me, Uriah. This is just a mistake. They'll get it figured out."

My thoughts were so dark and confused, I couldn't form a sentence. Her distress added to my own suffering. God knows I had inflicted her with much pain and tears over the years, but seeing her in such a state now was more than I could bear. I only wanted to end it all.

My memory about this time is extremely clouded. I was in such anguish that the days blended together into a dark blur. How could I be accused of attacking a teenaged girl? I kept reviewing the events of November 24, 2004.

That was the day before Thanksgiving, so it wasn't difficult to recall what I'd done. I woke in the nice little house I shared with my girlfriend and her son and prepared to go to work. The day began like any other in those days—with crystal meth. I smoked some in the living room, and then did a couple of lines for good measure as the drug no longer had the same effect on me as when I'd first started using it. Staying awake for days at a time was also taking its toll. My mind and body were getting worn out from such abuse. I was very thin with sores on my arms, legs, and face from the chemicals in the drug finding their way out through my pores.

I left for work around 6:30 and stopped at the Arco gas station for coffee and a PowerAid. Shortly before 7:00, I arrived at my jobsite in a warehouse on the extensive grounds of the Midway postal facility. We had done several jobs at Midway, and it was one of my favorite places to work. The Post Office itself was an old, concrete, three-story structure with a dark, musty-smelling basement that reminded me of the tunnels I'd loved exploring as a kid.

During the workweek prior to Thanksgiving, we'd been disassembling a mezzanine (a large frame used as a rack for storage), which we were going to transport to another USPS facility and reassemble there.

My girlfriend called my cell phone twice on Wednesday, after 11:00 AM but before noon, asking directions so she could pick me up for a quick lunch. After she arrived, she drove us to a taco shop adjacent to the property, on the opposite side of the post office and the warehouse. We ordered our food to go and drove to the end of the little shopping center, where we parked facing the postal property. We sat in the vehicle, eating and talking.

When I finished my burrito, I smoked some meth. Then she took me back to the jobsite. I was gone less than thirty minutes.

My co-worker and I continued taking apart the rack in the warehouse until between 3:00 and 3:30, when we parted company and wished each other a happy Thanksgiving. Rick and I spoke briefly about meeting the next day at my sister's house to enjoy Thanksgiving dinner with her family.

Over and over, I reviewed those events. How could I be accused of a crime in Lemon Grove, twelve miles and at least fifteen minutes from where I'd worked all day?

Memories of the time following that traumatic hearing elude me. But I can recall earlier events because the hearing didn't occur until some time after I'd arrived at San Diego Central Jail (SDCJ). The horrible booking process especially remains vivid.

I was taken from one overcrowded holding tank to another, each filthy and freezing cold. And each teeming with inmates—some reeking of body odor or booze, some obviously coming down from drugs or apparently deranged—many agitated and angry. Several fights broke out, mainly beatdowns. After ten or twelve hours, I was finally taken to a housing unit and put into a cell with a gray floor and block walls painted white. It was cold.

Shortly after my arrival, a detective paid me a visit and began to question me, but I told him I had nothing to say without an attorney present. I had no idea about the impending charges, although by then I'd heard the authorities suspected me of robbing someone. While these rumors caused me a little concern, I was not greatly worried because I knew I'd committed no such crime. I figured it was nonsense and would come to nothing. Later I would learn that the detective was the investigating officer on the sexual assault case.

Seventy-two hours after I arrived in San Diego, I was taken to court for an extradition hearing. No charges were mentioned, just the fact that I'd been extradited. The judge consulted with the attorneys and set a future court date. So even that gave me no hint about the horrible charges.

The aftershocks of that hearing left me feeling disoriented and isolated. The only windows on the seventh floor were slits of frosted glass. A little light came in, but I couldn't see outside at all. I felt as if I were in a spaceship, far away in another galaxy.

Dad and I spoke regularly on the phone, but he had experienced his own jail trauma for false accusations. He went ballistic when he heard about my charges, and became completely torn up whenever we spoke about my situation. Deep down, I knew—and Mom later confirmed—that his volatile emotions made him too unpredictable for a visit. My stepdad was still angry and didn't want anything to do with me. So Mom was the only person who came to see me, and all our visits were no-contact.

Through the thick glass and poor phone connection, she'd encourage me by saying things like, "I'm not giving up on you, Uriah, no matter what." Her comfort was good medicine for my shell-shocked soul.

The best medicine was my continued Scripture reading. I studied the Bible with a few older men, whose differing views fascinated me. I dove deeper into the Word to discover the truth. Becoming enamored with the Bible, I took up reading it each day like a farmer takes the plow in his hand, working from early morning until sundown. Only this was no burdensome task. It was a labor of love.

My increasing interest in Scripture is about the only thing I can be sure of during those black days. But I would soon discover the even greater darkness of incarceration in Vista.

8

Violent Environment

Vista Detention Center

I stood with a thin towel wrapped around my waist, waiting for the shower. A Southsider (Mexican gang member) walked in front of me as if he were going to get in before me.

I shuffled forward in my jail-issued flip-flops. "Hey, I'm next."

He glared. "Are you telling me when I'm getting in the shower?"

"No, I'm telling you when *I'm* getting in the shower."

He swore at me and then strode away.

Rather than take my turn, I dashed to my cell and told my cellie and another guy with him what had just happened.

Only about a minute later, a dozen Southsiders rushed our cell.

A large man threw a punch at me. I ducked and struck back. He landed a blow to my left eye. I shook my head, but kept swinging. Another guy ran at me and I kicked him in the groin. My towel was torn off in the melee, and I fought completely naked, kicking, punching, and taking blows. I was fighting for my life in nothing but my bare skin.

The deputies finally noticed the commotion. The alarm blared. A voice barked over the intercom. "Return to your cells immediately."

A little later, a couple of deputies took my cellie and me out of the module for a physical inspection. They examined us and took pictures of our faces and bodies. The damage was minimal, mostly bumps and abrasions, except for my black eye and my cellie's gouged forehead, where a chunk of meat had been cut out by a razor.

Being forced to fight naked taught me more of the many lessons I learned during my incarceration: never go to the shower wearing only a towel. Keep your shoes on at all times, even until you enter a shower (to this day I feel more secure when I'm wearing shoes). Watch what you say and how you say it.

The Vista facility of the county jail system was a violent place, and I absolutely hated it.

*

I was transferred to the San Diego County Jail in Vista at the beginning of April in 2005. Any transfer is disruptive to an inmate, even when it's for the better. And in my case, this move definitely was not.

Due to the nature of my charges, I was put in a high-power unit. That means I was housed with inmates who were either looking at hard time or were repeat offenders going back to prison—some for life—and many were gang members. These hardened criminals loved to prey on the weak.

I thought I had landed in hell.

My first cellmate in Vista gave me some much-needed schooling on doing time with such a crowd of violent predators. After a couple of weeks, he asked me, "What are you really in for?"

Completely taken off guard, I said, "Well, the kidnapping and robbery charges actually involved a teenaged girl." (I was smart enough not to mention rape.)

He raised his eyebrows. "Best keep that part to yourself for safety's sake."

We didn't talk about it again.

I have no idea why I shared even that much with him. I do know that God was protecting me. To see how amazingly he did that throughout my entire incarceration, you must understand the pecking order and politics in jails and prisons, especially in California, which has some of the most violent prisons in the nation. Gangs and racism are at the center of it all.

Every inmate who walks through the gate of the module must show his paperwork (listing his charges) to his shot caller, who is the white, black, or Hispanic rep. The shot caller for biracial gangs is their gang rep. Paperwork is always checked upon entering new digs, especially an already occupied cell. Everyone—at the very least the big dogs—knows what you're in for. But no one ever asked to see my paperwork, which is totally unheard of.

There is an unwritten rule that no child molesters or sex offenders are allowed to walk the mainline or be in general population. Inmates enforce that rule with utmost brutality. Because so many sexual offenders were being beaten or even killed, anyone now arrested for a sex crime is automatically put in protective custody by law.

But when I was booked, I was given the choice of going to protective custody (PC) or remaining in general population (GP). I made the decision to stay in GP based on horror stories I'd heard about PC during my past stints in jail. (Later I would learn the rumors were mostly false.) Having gotten away with hiding out thus far, I figured I'd continue my ruse—I was there for kidnapping and robbery, worthy things to be jailed for in inmates' minds.

Twice, I became a cellie with a white rep, neither of whom ever asked to see my paperwork. One of them even got me out of a potentially hazardous situation with the Southsiders. But no inmate would have protected me if the extent of my charges were discovered—as I witnessed with my own eyes.

One day I was distracted from reading in my cell by some nearby action. A middle-aged Mexican guy was being placed in the module. As he entered his assigned cell, a young Southsider stood beside the doorway and let him pass through. A little while later, more Southsiders rushed the cell. Screams and wails echoed from within. For long minutes, I listened in horror to a man pleading for the beating to stop, begging for his life. He was battered so brutally that when he crawled out of his cell, his form was mangled into a bloody mass.

Terror filled me at the thought of what would happen if the rape charge were ever discovered. I couldn't help feeling sorry for the guy even though he was charged with a sexual assault. Although the savagery doesn't continually haunt me, the image remains vivid when I recall the incident.

It was impossible to avoid violence in Vista. In addition to the life-threatening melee following the shower incident, I once fought two other white guys. A young inmate picked a fight with me, and his cellie attacked me from behind. That brawl left me with another blackened eye. I'm sure Mom's heart broke when she saw my second black eye, but all she said was, "Looks like you're going to have to learn to duck."

Not long after I'd arrived in Vista, I called Jessica one evening. She told me that she'd lost the baby, sobbing as she described the experience. Being unable to comfort her except for a few feeble words, I felt utterly helpless. Added to the infuriating injustice of being jailed for a crime I didn't commit, this seemed like kicking a man who already lay bleeding in the dirt.

I'm ashamed to admit that I coped with all this stress by continuing my addictions. I was able to obtain prescription drugs to get high and had learned the craft of making pruno (fermented prison wine). I still had the urge for meth, but I didn't touch it. The amount available wasn't sufficient for my satisfaction, and I had no desire to stay up all night while in jail. I preferred the oblivion of sleep.

But something else was happening, too. As a result of studying the Bible, I began to feel a strange sense of conviction mixed with fear. The son of disobedience, having been engulfed in moral, mental, and spiritual darkness his whole life, was finally learning that he was accountable to God.

Those feelings would not go away, although I tried my best to suppress them while continuing to indulge my addictions. Ignoring this new sense of conscience, however, would soon end.

One day I was called unexpectedly from my cell to the visiting room. On the other side of the glass, I saw Mom and my sister, Misty, whom I hadn't seen the entire time I'd been in jail, holding her infant daughter.

Misty already had three sons, and I smiled as she showed me her only, precious daughter. Olyvia was two months old, and I was thrilled to see her for the first time. When Misty handed the baby to Mom and sat down, I sensed something was wrong.

She picked up the phone and turned toward the glass. "Ry, I have something to tell you." Then she began sobbing. Finally, she said, "Kyng was killed by a drunk driver."

This news shook my very soul. I couldn't believe it, especially since I had recently begun saying a morning prayer asking the Lord to watch over my loved ones and keep them safe. Kyng was dead. How was that keeping him safe?

Misty, Mom, and I talked over the phones and shed many tears together. If only I could wrap my arms around my sister! Not only did I want to comfort her, but I needed comfort, too.

When it was time for me to leave, the reality of the loss hit me like a punch to the solar plexus. I made sure to leave the visiting area last, so the other inmates wouldn't see my face. As I approached the deputy at the door, he asked, "What's wrong, Uriah?"

I struggled to hold back the tears. "My brother-in-law, Kyng, was killed by a drunk driver."

He rubbed his chin and looked at me. "Would you like to go to the small recreation area outside for a while?"

I won't soon forget that act of kindness. In the yard, I walked in circles, sobbing freely. I didn't understand why God was allowing my family to experience such hardships. First, I was jailed wrongfully, and now my dear brother-in-law was killed by a drunk driver. What in the world was going on? I cried and poured out my heart to God. Why was he was putting us through so much turmoil? I railed at him in anger and confusion. I wanted answers.

None came that day. I finally willed myself to stop crying, so my eyes would dry out and my face clear up. Then I went back to my cell and lay on my bunk, facing the wall. My cellie let me be.

Because of my environment, I wasn't able to mourn Kyng's death naturally. Instead I kept it almost entirely inside. Kyng and I had spoken on the phone a couple of times while I was in jail, and I often reflected on those conversations. He'd been happy to hear that I was reading the Bible and had encouraged me to continue.

Two crucial things happened in the month after the Lord took Kyng home: I prayed "the sinner's prayer" and I gave up my addictions.

Reading the Bible three times a day had greatly encouraged, comforted, and strengthened me. But I hadn't attended chapel services. One evening soon after Kyng's death, a service was announced. I decided to go.

Although I have no recollection of what the Scripture was about, God convicted me that the hour had come to confess my sins and repent, to move from guilt to grace. At the end of service, we were told to bow our heads and pray with the worship leader. I did. I invited Christ into my heart. I asked him to forgive all my sins and help me trust Jesus as my Lord and Savior. That was at 9:15 p.m. on August 7, 2005.

My conscience, the soul's warning system, continued piercing my heart. How could I go on serving my fleshly desires when I daily read God's commands against them? It was foolish nonsense and showed that my heart was not right with God. Kyng was dead by the stupidity and carelessness of a drunk driver. Driving drunk was something I'd done for years and been arrested for twice. And here I was, sitting in jail, still getting inebriated. I decided to stop drinking and getting high. I asked the Lord to deliver me from my addictions. He did.

God removed my desires and gave me strength to resist many temptations. My sinful rebelliousness no longer controlled my life.

My Lord having saved my eternal soul, I endeavored to stop serving myself and start serving him. Since I was now in Christ, I needed to live a life pleasing and acceptable to God, and without reproach among my fellow inmates and especially with the sheriff's department. The last thing I needed was another charge added to the list I already faced. Around this time, I might even have become a bit legalistic.

Law was exactly what my rebellious heart needed. It's almost like I was wired for law, having been a lawbreaker my whole life. Plus, I was dealing with legalities on a very personal basis. Law was something I could relate to and certainly needed, but grace was completely foreign to me. The law said "do," and for a time I did, or at least tried to. I understood that I couldn't work for or earn my salvation, but I thought that if I did good works and lived a pure life, God would take notice and get me out of my terrible situation. In reality, I was asking God to be my magic genie in a bottle.

I became rigid and disciplined in my personal behavior and devotional practices, taking this—like everything I'd ever done—to the extreme. But I had inaccurate perceptions of the Christian life. What I needed was a good pastor or someone to teach me the Bible and the ways of God.

All I had ever known until this turning point was how to love and serve self. How was I to love God, especially when he seemed so distant? I say "seemed," because he was not far away at all. My conscience was just so seared that I was unable to sense the Lord's presence.

During this time, Jessica and Colton kept in contact. Whenever I heard Colton's voice on the phone, my spirit rose. This was my son, my own flesh and blood. Not having the ability to be near him—to touch him and look into those big, brown eyes and see his smiling face—was maddening. His face mirrored mine, only his conveyed innocence, while mine was marred by years of drug and alcohol abuse. I prayed often, asking the Lord not to allow my boy to be anything like his dad and to give him strength to stay away from drugs, alcohol, and sexual immorality.

Jessica and I made plans for marriage and a family, owning our own home, and all the other hopes and dreams people have, not even considering the Lord's will. I was desperate to have her and Colton in San Diego, so I could see them and be comforted by their nearness while dealing with my legal issues. Texas seemed as far away as the dark side of the moon.

My naiveté with regard to the legal system was setting me up for a great fall into the hands of Lady Justice herself. I truly believed that justice would prevail, that the truth would come out. Perhaps a detective would pay me a visit and say they made a mistake or they had caught the man who actually committed the crime.

Day after day, I dwelled on these and other possible scenarios, hoping and praying the Lord would rescue me. But days turned into months and months into over a year, and every day brought me closer to a trial.

Since I still had an attorney on retainer, I asked him to represent me. After he learned how serious the charges were, he decided to bring another attorney on board, one supposedly more experienced at handling such felony cases.

One day they visited me, and we talked about the case (and, of course, legal fees). Then the first one left. As soon as the door closed, the second attorney pulled a voice recorder from his pocket and turned it off, making some comment about covering his backside. So, right from the get-go, red flags waved in my face. But what was I to do? I needed someone to represent me, and I didn't want that to be what inmates call a "dump-truck" court-appointed attorney. The truth is some of them are very good, but I didn't realize it then. Financial considerations also loomed huge. My family had already paid them thousands of dollars, and we couldn't afford to start all over again.

I had a few court hearings during this time, but only the preliminary hearing stands out in my memory as it set my course and tested my new faith in Christ.

That morning, my rolling stomach refused food. This hearing would establish the charge and determine if there was a need for a trial. I hoped that the Lord would cause everything to go well and I would not have to stand trial on these terrible accusations. I prayed that the victim—whoever she was—would see me in person for the first time and tell the court she and the authorities had made a mistake.

A large Sheriff's Department bus, its rumbling engine spewing diesel fumes, waited in the pre-dawn dimness to take me on the forty-five minute ride to the downtown courthouse. I shuffled up the steps and into a seat, my wrists and ankles already aching from cuffs being fastened too tightly. But the tingling in my fingers was nothing compared to my mental torment.

As the bus drove down the I-5, the sun rose above the mountains. My eyes drank in the beauty of the ocean and marshes. I thought about all the places I'd been along that stretch of highway. I had worked on a post office with my stepdad in that city, and the one after it. I had gone with my family to that beach, and the next one.

Everything around me was so beautiful, and here I sat, going to a court hearing with an unpredictable outcome. It was like looking at the world through a telescope lens from another planet.

Court was in session. I sat between my attorneys at the defense table. I wore my prison blues, which my attorneys shouldn't have allowed, as it will automatically cause a witness to assume you're guilty. The victim was called into the courtroom, and after being sworn in, she took her seat at the witness stand. I looked at her, waiting for eye contact and her dawning realization that this was all a big mistake.

The prosecuting attorney asked, "Do you see in this courtroom today the man who attacked you?"

Her face turned toward me, but her eyes appeared to look through me. Oh, the wave of emotions that raced through me when we made momentary eye contact! I mentally pleaded with her to tell the truth and say it wasn't me.

"Yes," she said. "That's the man who attacked me."

I was crushed. All my prayers seemed to plummet from the heavens like boulders falling upon my head.

A little later, one of my attorneys asked, "Are you sure my client is the one who attacked you?" She said she was 80 percent sure. But that didn't matter. A trial court date was set, and I was shuffled off to the holding cells to wait for the bus ride back to Vista.

When it was time to leave, I was handcuffed again. My fingers and parts of my hands were still numb weeks later from those handcuffs being on so tightly.

On that return ride, I watched the sun fade into the ocean. Then all was dark—fitting for a mind filled with darkness and terror. But I asked the Lord to turn my thoughts from darkness to light. He did just that.

Was I angry? Absolutely. I experienced a multitude of emotions, far more than I can express in my meager vocabulary. I couldn't comprehend why all this was happening and felt I needed to make sense of this disaster.

My Bible reading never waned in those days of distress. The greater my anguish, the deeper and longer I dove into the Word. I also prayed more. I was learning that prayer takes discipline, patience, and denying of self—none of which I was accustomed to. Meditating on God and the Bible was easy, but actually speaking to God? That was altogether different. I had to chew the cud with God, communing *with* him, not simply talking *to* him. I knew a great deal about him, but I didn't actually know him yet. I was still speaking to a stranger, unsure of what to say and how to say it.

I developed a very structured prayer routine. My first prayer was while I lay awake until our cell doors unlocked around 7:00 or 8:00. When we were locked in our cells again for afternoon count, I'd sit on my rack and pray. Then when the cells were locked for the night, I'd have my third scheduled prayer. Many times throughout the day, I would shoot little prayers to the heavens like arrows, but those specified prayer times were irrevocable. Sometimes I had so much to say I couldn't wait. Other times, I acted like a recalcitrant child.

Twice a week, my mother drove forty-five minutes there and back to visit me. Despite the glass separating us, she and I grew closer than ever. We talked about our deepest, most sensitive thoughts and poured out our hearts.

Vista was a terrible place: overcrowded, extremely violent, and too far from my mama. It was also incredibly stressful for me to be shuffled back and forth from there to the downtown courthouse for every hearing.

I told my attorneys I needed to be moved back down to San Diego Central Jail or I'd go insane. They petitioned the court to have me transferred back, perhaps more for their own convenience than my personal welfare, but it was an answer to prayer in the Lord's timing and providence.

Sadly, my old sin nature would rear its ugly head and cause me excruciating suffering after my return to Central.

9

Temptation's Torment

San Diego Central Jail, 4th Floor

My mind filled with despair and my back throbbing with pain, I shuffled around the dayroom on Central's fourth floor. As usual, other inmates passed by without speaking to me. I agonized in my own private purgatory.

As I walked slowly back toward my cell, a skinhead who'd recently come in off the street spoke to me. "Hey, man."

I kept moving. "What's up?"

He fell into step beside me. "I hear you got a Bible."

Wondering what he was driving at, I replied, "Yeah, I do."

He lowered his voice. "I got some weed."

My gut wrenched. "So?"

"So if you give me a page to roll a joint, I'll let you smoke it with me."

My mind churned. Using a thin page from a Bible to roll a joint was a common practice in jail. I hadn't been high for a long time. And I was so terribly miserable.

I glanced around. No deputies were near. "Okay. Only I roll it."

The skinhead gave me the weed, but I gave in to my weakness and the devil's temptation. Satan set the hook, and I took the bait.

In my cell during afternoon lockdown, I prepared to roll the joint—all the while wrestling with my conscience. This was utterly sinful. How could I do such a thing with a page from a book that had become so dear?

But I was so depressed, I needed a lift.

What if we got caught? And I'd been sober for more than two months—why mess it up now?

It was only weed. Wouldn't it be wonderful to escape my hell for just a few moments?

In the end, the remnants of my sin nature held sway in the courtroom of conscience, and I fell headlong into temptation. I rolled the joint.

As soon as dayroom opened up, I went to the skinhead's cell and smoked the joint with him and another inmate. It had been almost a year since I'd smoked any pot, so it made me very stoned. We stood around chatting for a few minutes, and then I left to walk some laps in the dayroom.

The temporary escape I expected turned into a torture session. My nice little buzz transformed into a nightmare as I grew more and more paranoid. I expected the deputies to rush into the module any moment and slap the cuffs on me. Any time now an inmate would call me out on my rape charges. Then what? A severe beating—like the one I witnessed in Vista—or even death. My jaw clenched, and I began to hyperventilate. Many terrors raced through my mind as I walked around, but the worst was the horror I felt from sinning against God Almighty.

No longer able to stay in the dayroom, I fled to my cell for refuge and sank onto my bunk. Like Jonah, I thought I could flee from the Lord. I sat there, staring at the wall. How could I have been so foolish? Scripture text after text came to mind, confronting me with my sin. My throat constricted as shame washed over me. I felt so dirty, so unworthy of calling myself a Christian. This had been the exact opportunity Satan was waiting for. In a moment of weakness, I let my guard down, disobeying the living Word and its Author. Instead, I used the devil's logic to persuade myself it would be okay to get high. I loathed myself for thinking I could dance around the golden calf for a quick fix.

I stared at the grimy wall. I wished I could pull out one of those blocks, crawl inside, and die.

*

When the Lord delivered me from the turmoil and violence of Vista back to San Diego Central Jail in the fall of 2005, it was an answer to my fervent prayers. But my first weeks at Central were nothing like what I'd expected.

After hours in the cold and filthy processing tanks, I was placed on the fourth floor with inmates in the process of being transferred. Because it was a place of transition with a constant turnover of inmates, it was very unsettling—like living in a bus depot.

I was not permitted even the few items of personal property I'd had in Vista. My canteen (food and hygiene items I'd purchased), books (except for a blue Gideon Bible I'd picked up from the dayroom), and my accumulated mail had been thrown into a clear garbage bag and tossed into a closet on my floor. But I was not allowed access to them.

Time passed very slowly. No chapel services were available. The dayroom was open even less than I was accustomed to, but I was so depressed that I mostly stayed in my cell. All my sitting and stress caused severe back pain. I felt isolated and frightened. I was just plain miserable and desperately wanted off that floor.

I cried to the Lord to deliver me. Instead, my patience was stretched to its breaking point, my faith tried, and my obedience tested. I failed the test, but I paid the price in torment of soul.

Never before had my conscience felt so overwhelmed with guilt. When I set my mind's eye upon the heavens, all I saw was a frowning providence. When I looked inward, I saw only a condemning conscience. Sorrow upon sorrow filled my heart, and I pleaded with the Lord to forgive me. I had sinned against a holy and altogether righteous God, and for some time afterward I tasted sin's bitter fruits.

Only a week or so later another temptation arose. This time it was meth, my favorite drug. My new cellie said he had some.

"It's crystal." He walked to the metal table attached to the wall and sprinkled out the meth, glistening and enticing. I gazed at it. It was, indeed, crystal meth—shiny and glassy—and totally deceiving.

My cellie grinned. "You want to do a line with me?"

"No."

He raised his eyebrows. "That was quick. Sure you don't want some?"

I turned away. "No, I don't, man. I'm good. I'm trying to quit." Still shaken with fear from sinning against God just a short time earlier, I was not about to increase the weight upon my soul. Also, I really did want to stop using drugs. I was sick and tired of being dependent on a substance created by man to escape reality, and I was determined that the enemy within was not going to have its way.

My cellie shrugged. "Suit yourself." He snorted both lines.

The next day I had an appointment on a different floor, and when I returned to the fourth level, I asked the deputy if I could be moved to another cell. Surprisingly, he said, "Yes." About an hour later, he moved me.

These types of temptations were prevalent throughout my entire incarceration. If you wanted a particular drug, it could easily be purchased. Either white lightning (alcohol) or plain old pruno (wine) could be bought or made on your own. Prescription drugs and tobacco, although illegal to possess or use in California jails and prisons, were also available. If you had the money or knew the right people, your particular vice could be obtained. The barter system is still widely used in this day and age in America. Coffee, stamps, and ramen soups equal currency in the prison system.

But God was ever faithful to provide escape from temptation (1 Cor 10:13). Embracing that verse and all the other promises I discovered in the written Word, I was empowered by the Holy Spirit not to fall prey again to the devil's dainty little treats. That joint I smoked with the two inmates would be the last time I ever got high.

Shortly thereafter, I spoke to a psychologist. I told him I was preparing for trial on serious charges, which were causing me much emotional anguish, and being stuck on the fourth floor exacerbated my mental distress. I was promptly moved to the sixth floor.

I'd been desperate to be moved to a module with less stress and more stability. The Lord, knowing my frailty, gave me exactly that.

10

Painful Progress

San Diego County Jail, 6th Floor

The loudspeaker in the dayroom crackled: "Chapel services are being held."

My heart leaped. I'd only been on the sixth floor for a few days, and this was the first time I'd heard the call for chapel.

The deputy continued, "If you'd like to attend, write your name on the sign-up sheet when it is distributed to your module."

Earlier, a couple of other inmates had told me the services here were pretty good. When the list came around to D module, I signed up.

About ten or fifteen minutes later, a deputy stood in the dayroom doorway and called the names of those who had signed the sheet, including, "Uriah Courtney."

I joined the few inmates lining up along the glass wall beside the module. The deputy escorted us to a small adjacent room. Near the door stood a gentle-looking old man, slightly stooped, with white hair.

He smiled and put out his hand. "Hello, there. I'm Chaplain Budlove."

I shook his hand and felt comforted by his touch. "My name is Uriah."

His eyes sparkled behind his glasses. "Like Uriah the Hittite in the Bible?"

"Exactly." I felt an immediate connection. I turned to greet a petite elderly woman with a heartwarming smile. She reached up and embraced me in an affectionate hug. "My name is Erma, but most of the boys call me Mom."

That was the first time I'd been hugged in over nine months. It felt wonderful. Mom Budlove hugged me every time I attended chapel services. I don't think any of the guys ever turned down a hug from Mom.

I don't recall the topic of that first sermon, but I'll never forget the Budloves' compassion. They truly lived up to their last name, mirroring the love of Christ by loving every brother unconditionally.

Each week Pastor Budlove preached about sin, hell, repentance, and the necessity of believing in Jesus Christ in order to be saved from your sins. His sermons affected me deeply.

During the week, the Budloves made their rounds to the modules. A deputy would open the little security slot in the door, so they could deliver Bibles or other materials an inmate had requested. I often asked Chaplain Budlove about biblical matters or a particular concern. He would respond with Scripture or offer his sanctified common sense. He always ended with prayer.

How those prayers strengthened my faith! They increased my resolve to fight the good fight and not allow my circumstances to become a stumbling block in my spiritual progress. The Budloves' devotion to each other changed how I viewed marriage. Their interaction showed their respect and love for one another, and I longed for the same thing some day.

*

By the first week of November in 2005, when I was moved to the sixth floor, I had been in county jail for nine months. During that entire time, my senses—and sometimes my body—had been assaulted by extreme violence: vicious attacks, severe beatings, racial hatred, and gang drama that frequently escalated to fights and melees. The sixth floor in D module was much different. While fights and an occasional drug overdose or suicide still occurred, there was little gang or racial tension. As in previous locations, inmates governed themselves by unwritten codes, but the ones in my new module were commonsense rules essential for keeping the peace.

The sixth floor housed inmates with psychological issues and about as many without mental problems. I think I fell somewhere in between (I wish you could see my grin as I write that). Many men faced life sentences, most of them accused of murder. A couple would become close companions, but I guarded the amount of personal or legal information I revealed to even them.

Although I didn't suffer from claustrophobia, I hated being confined and unable to leave of my own volition. It made me feel like the large cats

I used to watch at the San Diego Zoo, pacing back and forth with a weary and hungry look in their eyes.

From my cell on the upper tier of D module, I could see the clock on the wall outside the dayroom. Even though it seemed like the world clock had ceased turning, I knew that time hadn't stopped. Being able to check the hour of the day allowed me to organize my life in a very structured—almost militaristic—manner.

I continued my practice of designating specific time slots for personal Bible study and prayer. To get in shape, I performed 500 push-ups every morning and another 500 each evening. It sounds like a lot, but it's not that hard once you condition your body. And I had plenty of time.

Seeking other productive activity, I took all the classes I could: Adult Basic Education (ABE), AIDS Awareness, Anger Management, Alcoholics Anonymous, Narcotics Anonymous, Drug Education Group, Domestic Violence, and Parenting. I learned some great information from AA and NA, but after a while I could no longer listen to the stories of addiction experiences. Personally I was ashamed of my past and didn't care to talk about it at every meeting. To me, it seemed like glamorizing a sinful life and felt like a dry high. I'm not condemning AA or NA—thank God so many people have found a way to get and stay sober through these organizations—but I wanted to depend more on God and the Scriptures to maintain sobriety.

The class I most enjoyed was ABE. When I first attended, the teacher helped me with basic math as well as geometry, which fascinated me. Maybe it was because, without realizing it, I'd been using geometry's principles in the past when I framed houses and in other areas of construction. Now I learned the meaning and purpose for all those angles, points, and lines. But I felt frustrated that I couldn't apply what I was learning out on a jobsite.

Later I discovered a cabinet containing a complete set of Encyclopedia Britannica. I buried myself in those great books. I traveled the world, met fascinating people, and explored important historical sites. I read or browsed each page and eventually worked through the entire set. More than once, I went through the set again, rereading things that captured my interest. I cherished those books because they taught me many things and provided a healthy escape from incarceration's monotony.

The lack of sensory stimulation and physical activities made every day repetitive and dull, even though I experienced extreme physical, emotional, and spiritual highs and lows.

Years of substance abuse had turned my body into a bag of bones, and I suffered ailments ranging from ingrown toenails to a nasty infection after having a wisdom tooth extracted. I had complained for days about the pain and continuous bleeding, but it wasn't until my face grew disfigured from swelling that the guards could no longer ignore my pleas for medical attention. Two huge sheriff's deputies shackled me and sandwiched me between them while I was taken to an outside hospital for treatment.

Fear for my life created constant tension in my body and mind. I never knew when my charges might be revealed or when I might be attacked. I felt as if I walked on eggshells.

I always slept on the top bunk because I felt safer. That higher angle would make it more difficult for an attacker to inflict injury and give me more of a fighting chance. But even the top bunk couldn't protect me from a quick and fatal strike, like a slit to the throat or blow to the head. This wasn't pure paranoia. Life-threatening assaults occur all the time in jails and prisons, especially to sex offenders.

Anger over my unjust incarceration burned within me like a hidden river of lava, ready to erupt. Each court hearing fueled my internal fire. Time after time I sat in the courtroom, listening to the powers that be exchange all manner of legal jargon that sounded like a foreign language. I continually suppressed the urge to jump out of my seat and scream that this was all bullshit and I didn't do any of the things they were talking about. The fire inside was raging out of control and turning into an inferno.

My spiritual state was a roller coaster ride of plummeting doubt and ascending assurance. The concept of the Trinity created a long struggle.

Because this doctrine mystified me, I began studying the Bible with a Jehovah's Witness, curious to know what he believed. As we studied verses that seemed to discredit the concept of the Trinity, I began to reject it. My main reason was simple, yet illogical. The word *Trinity* was nowhere in the Bible. How could I believe something that wasn't given a name in Scripture? Other Christian doctrines were named (sanctification, justification, election, etc.), so I could easily affirm them. But not Trinity. This was unacceptable to me.

Then my Bible study partner began to attack the divinity of Christ, raising more doubts in my mind. He had slipped false teaching into our Bible study like barely felt tremors, but his heresy shook the foundational truths of my Christian faith as much as a major earthquake. I spent months poring over Scripture in search of verses validating the Trinity and Jesus as

God. In the end, I came to a comfortable acceptance that Jesus is God and that he exists as the second person in the Trinity, distinct from God the Father and the Holy Spirit, yet the three are really one.

The most meaningful books in all my extensive Bible study were Job and the Psalms. Job's humble submission to God's sovereignty intrigued me. The parallels between his suffering and mine were many. He lost all his children to death. I lost Colton, or actually, I was lost to Colton.

Job endured severe physical afflictions and asked God why he was suffering. That very question was a constant theme in my prayers. Because there was no rational explanation for this disaster, I reasoned there must be a theological one. In the book of Job, I discovered pieces to this perplexing puzzle. God ordains that his beloved children suffer. This helped explain the mystery of pain and proved that God was in control, which comforted and strengthened me. I didn't have it all figured out, or I wouldn't have grumbled and wavered in my faith. But God eventually enabled me to comprehend that we must submit to his authority and confess with our friend Job, "The Lord gave, and the Lord has taken away; blessed be the name of the Lord" (Job 1:21), and, "I know that my Redeemer lives" (Job 19:25).

Job taught me much, but so did the Psalms. They were my spiritual food and drink, like milk and honey to a malnourished soul. They taught me how to pray, expressing complaints without sinning or simply enjoying communion with God. Because those in Christ are God's children, he desires to hear their voice. I longed to hear my son's voice every day, and I imagined it was the same for my heavenly Father.

The Psalms also taught me how to deal with daily reality. By the Spirit's grace, God helps the believer respond to real-life situations in praise or lament. Living in such a hostile environment and waiting for what seemed the day of my execution, I identified with cries against actions of the wicked as well as grief over personal propensity to sin. My life felt out of control, but God is sovereign and acts according to his own timetable. It was folly for me to expect him to invade time and space to miraculously deliver me.

The entire collection of Psalms is one thematic masterpiece from the Author of life and Creator of the universe. Some psalms, however, resonate more with me, particularly King David's laments. Perhaps because I share the rather unusual name of a man closely associated with this Israelite king (even though David sinned grievously against Uriah), I feel an affinity with David and his songs.

Despite David's sinfulness, God called him a man after his own heart. That comforted and encouraged me, because it showed God's great forgiveness and the hope for even a depraved sinner like me. King David's psalms paralleled my circumstances so closely, it seemed they had been written only for me. Pangs of distress sometimes overwhelmed me to the point my body felt completely wasted away. Psalm 22:14–15 described my agony quite vividly: "I am poured out like water, and all my bones are out of joint; my heart is like wax; it is melted within my breast; my strength is dried up like a potsherd, and my tongue sticks to my jaws; you lay me in the dust of death." Such laments perfectly expressed my emotions, but no matter how bitter, angry, or confused the psalmist began his lament, he always ended it on a faithful note by proclaiming the Lord's goodness and righteousness. Meditating on God's precious attributes was important for shaping my spiritual attitude.

Another crucial influence was evening prayer time. Every night, about an hour before lockdown, a brother named Sean would holler, "Prayer call." All who felt compelled would gather in a circle on one side of the dayroom. Once in a while, someone else led us in prayer. Occasionally that someone would even be me.

At first, Sean asked me in advance. Then he began to call on me then and there. This forced me out of my shell and made me reflect on the tribulations of others. I wasn't the only one dealing with personal calamity—so was everyone around me. I began to take an interest in new inmates and tried to steer them in the right direction.

These activities helped me assess my internal inferno. How could I lead prayer circle and mentor other young men fresh off the street while I had a heart full of anger and vengeance? My conscience let me know I was playing the hypocrite and dancing to the devil's tune in this unfolding drama.

I wanted to hold on to anger and other intrinsic dispositions because at least they made me feel something other than numbness. But God says, "Vengeance is mine, I will repay" (Rom 12:19, Heb 10:30). The Holy Spirit used that truth to begin to quench the fire within me.

Ephesians 4:26 especially affected me: "'Be angry, and do not sin.' Do not let the sun go down on your wrath." By comparing other texts, I realized that it was not always sinful to be angry. It would only be sinful if I remained in that state for a prolonged period of time, or if some ulterior motive drove my anger. Of course I was angry. I had been unjustly accused of a crime, while the actual perpetrator remained free, possibly committing more assaults. But I was feeding off anger to sustain a sinful feeling, rather than depending on God to feed my spiritual senses. I was "letting the sun go down on my wrath" and in danger of anger giving birth to bitterness. I needed to properly understand the difference between righteous indignation at injustice or evil, and a vengeful anger at the purveyors of it.

Of all the things my soul experienced through my spiritual progress, this was perhaps the fastest and least painful. God comforted me and enabled me to rest in his promises that vengeance is his alone. He is angry at the wicked every day. My duty was to be faithful to God and to leave all else in his capable hands.

For sixteen months, D module on the sixth floor was my home, my place of pain and my house of joy. I experienced moments of spiritual ecstasy, but I also wrestled against the spiritual forces of evil. These months also included relentless stress leading up to, during, and after my trial.

11

Pre-Trial Anxiety

San Diego County Jail, 6th Floor

My cellie left for the dayroom. As soon as he was out of sight, I ripped the corner from the sheet on which I'd been scribbling and tucked the scrap of paper into my sock. Then I slipped the legal pad under my mattress. I cleared my papers and books from the table and put them on my shelf. Rick would visit soon, and I wanted to be ready to leave as soon as I was called out.

Rick's compassion for Mom had eventually led him to start alternating visits with her. Those initial visits with Rick had been awkward, but once he realized that my charges weren't going away, he began to delve into the legal issues. The closer my trial drew, the more determinedly he pursued justice.

"Courtney," the call box crackled. "You've got a visitor."

In the visitation center, I found the booth with Rick on the other side of the glass. I picked up the phone. "Hi, Rick. Thanks for coming."

His voice crackled over the line. "Hi, Uriah. How did your hearing go this week?"

I shuddered. "Terrible. I don't understand half of what those attorneys say. Except for when the DA reads her papers. She says, 'Courtney this' and 'Courtney that' all the time, describing me doing these horrible things when I wasn't even there."

"I know better than anyone how wrong that is." Rick nodded. "You were working all day for me on November 24."

My hand clenched into a fist. "How did it get this far, Rick? How can I be going to trial for something I didn't do?"

"Just calm down, Uriah."

"How can I? This isn't the way it's supposed to be." I pounded the counter. "I should be considered innocent until proven guilty, but everyone acts like I'm guilty."

"I know they do, Uriah. But be careful what you say to your mom. She's in her own prison, thinking about you in here, and she doesn't need to hear your negative thoughts." He pulled a paper from his pocket and unfolded it. "Let's talk about something else. Listen to what this theologian wrote on free will."

His voice droned on, but his earlier words had reminded me of a recent conversation with Mom. When we spoke about my addictions and arrests, she'd broken down in tears. She'd wondered what she could have done differently and blamed herself for letting me live with my father. I'd tried to assure her that she was not at fault for how I turned out. I was responsible for my own actions.

While my dad certainly wasn't a good influence on me, he'd always been dealing with his own demons and he's not to be blamed either. It would be easy to blame one's parents or lack of them, the environment one grew up in, bad teachers, or society—whatever—for our own personal problems. When it really comes down to it, we're all responsible for our choices. A child's environment can make him more susceptible to substance abuse, but the actual root of any addiction is sin. I was born with a sin nature and I made conscious decisions that took me far down the wrong path.

I hoped and prayed for the opportunity to help my son make wise decisions and avoid the mistakes I'd made.

Now Rick said, "So what do you think?"

I tried to recall anything he'd just been saying. "About what?"

"About free will? You think he's right?"

"I'm not sure. I guess I'd have to read the article and study what the Bible says."

"Okay. I'll make a copy and send it to you."

"That would be great." I tried to focus on Rick. "How are things going for you? What jobs have you been working on?"

He launched into a detailed account of the past week's work with his other two employees, and my mind slipped back to being on a jobsite. I imagined the sound of a drill motor whirring, the shriek of a saw blade ripping through lumber, nail guns popping, hammers banging away. I could almost smell the sweet scent of sawdust and that musty smell of freshly poured cement.

He finished his story, and I sighed. "I miss working. I never thought I'd miss it so much."

"We miss you, too, Uriah." He cleared his throat. "I've been thinking about your trial—"

"Me, too. That's about all I ever think about." I reached down to pull the slip of paper from my sock. I held it against the glass with my hand covering it.

Rick's eyes scanned the text, which read: "What about my cell phone records? Have the attorneys considered those?"

Sometimes I asked case-related questions on notes because I didn't want inmates or deputies to overhear legal aspects of my trial.

Rick finished reading the note and glanced up. "My understanding is that they've checked into that and haven't found anything helpful."

I crumpled the paper scrap in my hand. "What about Jessica and Colton? Any progress there?"

Rick nodded. "I think so. We've got a room ready for them, and she's making plans to fly to San Diego."

For the first time in long while, I smiled. "Good. I can't wait for them to get here."

*

Jessica and Colton finally arrived and lived with Mom and Rick for awhile. This pleased me because I wanted my parents to get to know my future wife and their grandson. Jessica found a job and eventually moved with Colton into a little apartment only a few blocks from my parents' house and a short walk from the shore. Colton loved the beach. Jessica and my parents took many pictures, which they'd print out and mail or bring along during visits and hold up to the glass of the booth.

Having them near and being able to see them again was great, but bittersweet. I couldn't hug them or speak to them face-to-face. And Colton's understanding of the situation both amused and saddened me.

When Jessica would get ready for a visit, Colton would ask where they were going. She'd say, "We're going to see Daddy." He started calling the jail "Daddy's house." It broke my heart because he thought this was normal, but it made me happy that he understood our relationship.

During our visits, Jessica and I talked about our future, and I felt hopeful. Only one obstacle stood in the way of all our hopes: I was preparing for trial to fight a life sentence. The fear of the unknown caused enormous stress and anxiety in our hearts, which began to drive us apart.

Intense emotional torments smothered me. I felt as if I'd been forced to make my bed in hell and pull a blanket of dirt over my head.

The nearer my trial date approached, the more worry and fear plagued me. I agonized over every little detail I could glean from my attorneys or one of numerous court hearings. Many motions had to be filed as the attorneys strived for or against a host of things that could be either detrimental or preferential to my case. The legal battle was ugly, stressful, and confusing. I felt like a puppet, controlled by a vicious master, on a stage arranged to look like a courtroom.

In those days, I was a grumbler and a malcontent, venting my dissatisfaction. "Why won't you just do this or that, God? Why, why, why?"

As if I could actually do things better than the Lord or had the slightest clue as to what was in my best interests. Reviewing my life proves my point. I had gone my own way for years, spiraling downward into an abyss of debauchery and lawlessness. Uriah's way leads to death and destruction. God's way leads to life and eternal security.

Having wandered in the wilderness my entire life, I now saw for the first time God's promised inheritance of spiritual rest just over the horizon. But it appeared so distant.

I knew I was called to suffer and submit, but I didn't want to suffer. And the concept of submission was completely foreign. It seemed akin to giving up, a weakness or character flaw. I wanted to hold on to my little island of self-will and autonomy.

My island was an isle of lawlessness created by a man "depraved in mind and deprived of truth" (1 Tim 6:5). And I had been transformed by the renewal of my mind through the power of the Holy Spirit. My island had to go. The only way to annihilate it was full submission to God.

One day I read 1 John 5:14, "And this is the confidence we have toward him, that if we ask anything according to his will he hears us." That verse struck a forceful blow to my sensibilities. Was my specific prayer for exoneration aligned with the will of God?

I stared at the wall in my cell. That cold, white-painted cinder block resembled the impregnable, impenetrable wall of God's will I had just run up against. I tried to understand what this verse might mean with respect to the outcome of my trial. The psalms often speak of God's love for justice (e.g., Pss 33:5, 37:28, and 99:4), and I thought, *Surely God loves to see justice done on earth.*

For weeks I meditated on those words: "If we ask anything according to his will, he hears us." When I walked around the dayroom, when I prayed on my bed, when I read the Bible, when I visited with Mom or Rick, those words hung before my mind's eye like a plaque on a wall. How could I know if my prayer for justice accorded with God's will?

I couldn't. That realization was very difficult to accept. I desired to be free and nothing else. In effect, I was insisting God do something for me that might not be according to his will. I was committing sin against the sovereign Lord of the universe, like a petulant child disobeying his parents. It was my duty to seek God's will and his desires alone, "Not as I will, but as you will" (Matt 26:39).

After agonizing over this for many weeks, I finally submitted and prayed from then on, "Father God, you know my heart's desires, for you know all things. I just want to go home and get married, raise my son, go back to work, and attend a good church. Please cause the truth to be made known to the jury so that I may be exonerated of any and all wrong-doing. Nevertheless, O Lord, not my will, but yours be done. In Jesus name, I pray. Amen."

My lips uttered similar prayers day after day until and during my trial, and I confess I wasn't greatly comforted. But whether I liked it or not—whether I was comforted or not—was beside the point. The important thing was my submission and obedience to God, trusting in the promise "that for those who love God all things work together for good, for those who are called according to his purpose" (Rom 8:28).

One day my attorney came to see me. He straightened his tie. "Listen, Uriah. The prosecuting attorney and I met, and she said she'd be willing to accept a plea bargain."

"Plea bargain?"

"Yeah." He cleared his throat. "You agree to a guilty plea and you'll get only fifteen years."

"No way." I stood. "I'm not accepting a plea bargain for something I didn't do."

There was no escaping this trial now. All I could do was pray for a favorable outcome by a fair and sensible jury of my peers.

I spent a lot of time pleading with the Lord to cause my trial to go in my favor. Mary washed the Lord's feet with her tears, but I might have washed his entire body with mine.

12

Trial Trauma

San Diego County Courthouse

The morning of my trial finally arrived: February 24, 2006. As I lay on my rack, I felt so helpless. I knew I was innocent, but how could I prove it?

A deputy's voice echoed from the call box inside my cell at 4:30 a.m. "Courtney, prepare for court."

I raced to put on my jail blues, brush my teeth with the two-inch toothbrush, and stash my pocket Bible in my sock.

The door slid open and a deputy met me. He escorted me to the elevator and then to a holding cell on the second floor. Despite the early hour, my high-strung nerves felt like guitar strings about to break. I paced back and forth, praying and thinking about what I faced.

Due to my arrest record, I couldn't testify in my own defense. Although I had no history of violence toward women and had never committed a sexual offense of any kind, the prosecution would have brought up my past to persuade the jury those alcohol and drug charges were crimes of moral turpitude, and I had progressed to sexual assault.

My record was also the reason no witness could speak in support of my true character. The jury would hear only that I was a vicious monster, a sexual predator who had attacked a sixteen-year-old girl. *How could the jury make the right decision if they weren't going to hear the truth, the real story?* My heart was so heavy that I felt like the walking dead.

After about an hour, a different deputy escorted me to another holding cell, where inmates were permitted to change into street clothes for their court hearings or trials. I donned a cheap used suit provided by my attorney.

After a short time, the cell door slid open, and a deputy motioned for me to come out. "Let's go, Courtney." He escorted me to another holding cell. "Wait here until the courthouse opens."

A couple of other inmates already sat there in their dress-outs, staring through the glass windows overlooking the hallway, where literally hundreds of inmates filed past for their court hearings. Truly it was a mass of fallen, broken humanity herded like cattle to the slaughterhouse.

Eventually we were escorted to holding cells in the courthouse itself. For hours, I sat in the ill-fitting gray suit in a cold and dimly-lit holding tank.

The only other time I'd worn a suit had been for Misty and Kyng's wedding, when I had the honor of giving her away. Now I wore a suit that wasn't nearly as nice, and instead of escorting my sister down a bright aisle with her hand on my arm, I'd shuffled along a shadowy hall with shackles around my ankles, wrists, and waist. Rather than anticipating a marriage celebration and welcoming a new member into my family, I faced an unknown and foreboding future of isolation from everyone I loved.

I couldn't bear the idea of never again smelling campfire smoke and laughing with my family while enjoying Dad's spicy chili or Rick's delicious fish tacos. Thoughts of losing my future with my son were even more excruciating: to never see him play in the sand, never hear him shriek in the surf, or never hold his hand while the waves tugged at our feet.

I prayed and recited psalms, but my entire body trembled.

Finally, a deputy came to the door. "Courtney?"

"Yes." I stood and tried to keep my balance on shaky legs.

That deputy handed me off to the bailiff, who did a pat-down. He discovered my pocket Bible in my sock. "You know that's considered contraband, and it's not allowed in the courtroom."

"Yes, sir, but it's just a Bible."

Without saying anything more, he stuck it back in my sock.

He led me down long halls and up a couple flights of stairs to the courtroom. It was empty, except for my attorneys and the DA. The bailiff removed my shackles and I sat between my two lawyers.

Then he opened the courtroom doors. Mom rushed into the room and sat directly behind me. I wasn't supposed to, but I turned to her and said, "I love you, Mom."

Before the trial could begin, a jury had to be selected. That process completely disheartened me. I couldn't believe how many people in the jury pool either were involved with law enforcement or were related to someone who was. I felt that would automatically prejudice them against me.

My attorneys and the DA clashed over the selection of every juror. Once that mighty combat was over, the battle for my life began.

The judge read lengthy instructions to the jury: what was expected of them, not to discuss the case with anyone or even among themselves prior to deliberations, how to consider the facts and to not let any bias influence their decision.

Then the judge read aloud the charges. I watched the jurors' faces and wondered what they were thinking. Did they already think I had committed this crime since I sat here at the defense table? *Why else would he be sitting there, right? He must have done something wrong. Innocent people don't get accused of things they didn't do, because our system just doesn't work that way. This is America.*

My mind played tricks on me. I was terrified. I already felt defeated and convicted. So ended the first day.

*

If you've ever experienced a life-threatening moment, try to imagine that absolute terror—consuming and unremitting—for three full weeks. That's how long my trial lasted; three weeks of constant horror and hopelessness, interspersed with spikes of rage. Even now, trying to recall those traumatic days fills me with anxiety.

Time stood still for me as I suffered through this seemingly endless ordeal. My extremely distressed state during my trial prevents me from relating for sure who testified on what day. Some things, however, remain vivid.

Later I learned the reason it took so long for me to be called into the courtroom that first day was because my attorney refused to consent to a string of proposed judges. Apparently, it was difficult to find one with whom he didn't already have a negative history. The judge he finally settled on was a former cop and prosecutor. The District Attorney was married to a policeman. This all seemed very unfair and highly prejudicial, and the odds seemed already stacked against me.

On the second day of my trial, both the prosecution and the defense laid out their cases before the jury. According to the DA, I was a predator who had sexually assaulted a sixteen-year-old girl. The DA was very dramatic and persuasive. "I promise to provide evidence, ladies and gentlemen, primarily eyewitness identification by the victim herself as well as another person, to prove beyond a reasonable doubt that Uriah Courtney committed this terrible act."

My heart sank. It rose a little when my attorney summarized counsel's plan for presenting a two-part defense, based on misidentification and an alibi that I was working at the time the incident occurred.

The victim was the first person called to testify. I'll call her Allison to protect her privacy. She related the events of November 24, 2004, often dissolving into tears.

She'd left home that day around 11:45 to walk to a friend's house. She carried a CD player with a music disc inside. As she approached a Seven-Eleven convenience store on a corner, she noticed a white male staring at her from a light-colored pickup. She again noticed the driver looking at her as he drove through the parking lot.

After she crossed under a freeway overpass and began to walk up a hill, someone grabbed her from behind. Holding her with one arm in a viselike grip, the man reached down and pulled on her skirt and underwear, tearing them. She fought to get away, and he shouted in her left ear. She swung the CD player with her right hand and hit him in the face. His grip loosened, and she managed to break free, running into the street.

She didn't get far before her assailant again grabbed her from behind. He picked her up off her feet and dragged her back across the street as she kicked and screamed, losing both sandals and dropping her CD player. He flung her down in bushes next to the sidewalk. Throwing himself on top of her, he again ripped at her clothing and penetrated her vagina with his finger.

She kept fighting and broke free again. She ran back into the street where she flagged down a passing vehicle driven by an elderly woman. She got into the car. She and the woman watched as the man picked up her CD player, tossed out the disc, then ran down the street. The woman drove under the bridge, and the victim testified that she saw the assailant turn left at the light to head north, away from the back side of Home Depot. She described him as wearing shorts and a light grey T-shirt with an image on the front.

The woman driver insisted on following him, but he disappeared into the commercial buildings on that street. The woman then took the victim home, where the girl called police and showered. Two San Diego County

Sheriff's deputies and an investigating officer responded to her house. Then she was taken to a hospital for a sexual assault examination. (Because this was a digital rape and the victim had showered, DNA testing matched only the victim's profile.)

By this time, I'd heard most details of Allison's horrific experience, but during my trial I noticed some discrepancies with what she'd said at the preliminary hearing.

At the preliminary hearing, she had testified she was unable to get a "whole look" at the man, and that she was more confident in her identification of the truck than her attacker. Yet, at the trial, she testified she got a good look at the man while she fought back, seeing his face six times. She identified me as the assailant, but she said that on the day of the attack I was heavier, had shorter hair, and was clean shaven. (At trial I weighed around 175–180 pounds, more than at any time in my life, while on the day of the attack, I supposedly weighed approximately 150 pounds and had facial hair.)

The DA led Allison through hours of compelling and tearful testimony. How would sympathetic hearers believe she could be mistaken in identifying her attacker?

One of my attorneys questioned Allison for only about thirty minutes. I didn't want him to cause her suffering, but I felt he didn't ask the right questions and allowed her to set the direction. Yet the judge called for a recess, during which he admonished my attorney to take note of his tactics and suggested he rephrase his questions so as not to "badger" the witness.

The so-called badgering may have been perceived because the victim constantly qualified her testimony. It seemed she had been coached to state that my attorney was taking something "out of context" whenever he tried to point out discrepancies. She'd also evidently been told to constantly affirm her "good look" at the assailant and her conviction that it was me.

My attorney appeared incompetent, and the judge made him look worse. Forget about everything not looking so good leading up to the trial. This was The Trial, and we were off to a terrible start. My heart plummeted, and my other attorney took over from then on.

One thing that soon became evident was the extreme antagonism between this attorney and the DA, as well as between him and the judge. It must have been obvious to everyone in the courtroom, including the jurors. With sickening regularity, the DA's objections were sustained, while my attorney's objections were overruled. Every time that happened, nausea flooded my stomach in strong waves.

The attorneys or judge constantly called sidebars, during which matters were discussed in the judge's chambers or outside the hearing of the jurors in the courtroom. On a number of occasions, the jury left the room because a major issue arose, such as the lawyers arguing or something said in front of the jury that shouldn't have been. A bell rung that can't be un-rung.

Each conjecture "accidentally" revealed to the jury in this way infuriated me. Rage flared like a forest fire in my head.

At the time, I was especially angry at the second eyewitness, who hadn't bothered to stop to help a young woman in distress and hadn't come close to the perpetrator, yet felt qualified to identify him.

As this man drove past the scene, he initially noticed two people struggling in the bushes. He claimed he thought it was a couple having an argument (although he did admit seeing the man jerk up the girl's skirt). He witnessed the girl get into the woman's vehicle and the perpetrator pick up a baseball cap, which he held over his face. This second witness testified to seeing the assailant flee on foot back under the bridge and turn right at the next stop light, heading south behind the Home Depot store. He described the assailant as wearing jeans and a white T-shirt. This description of the attacker varied greatly from the victim's testimony, and his account of the direction the perpetrator ran was completely opposite. Although this man was about seventy or eighty feet from the scene, he identified me from a biased photo lineup put together by the investigating officer.

Explanation: an investigating officer shouldn't present the photo lineups as he could inadvertently (or intentionally) persuade the victim or eyewitness to pick someone they're unsure about or the person the cop believes is guilty. A person will often pick someone in a lineup simply because they want to please the officer. To help ensure accurate identification, photo lineups should be "double blind sequential," which means that the person showing the photos should not know which is the suspect and should show one after the other. But for both the victim and the other eyewitness, the investigating detective himself presented the photo lineup and showed six pictures at the same time.

During the trial, additional matters seemed mishandled outside the courtroom with this witness. My attorney later told me someone overheard a conversation between the witness and a person who appeared to be a detective. This person told the witness that Courtney was a "big-time drug dealer." He responded that it was a good thing he hadn't followed him then. This incident actually came before the judge, but not before the jury. My attorney argued that this exchange unfairly biased the eyewitness against me and sought a mistrial, but that was denied.

Another time someone saw the DA approach this witness and ask if he'd received the notes she'd sent him. When he responded negatively, she appeared irritated and sent someone to get a copy. Then she shoved the papers at him and told him those were the questions she was going to ask him and the answers she wanted him to say, telling him to make sure he read them. When this incident was brought to the judge's attention, the DA called the papers "transcripts" and stated that the witness wanted another copy, so she sent for them. The eyewitness confirmed receiving transcripts of his preliminary hearing testimony in preparation for his trial testimony, and the judge gave the DA a slight rebuke. To me, however, this appeared very much like coaching the witness and didn't seem right.

Evidence was presented that the DA showed the eyewitness my photo the morning before he was asked to identify the perpetrator. And that the DA, the eyewitness, the victim, and her mother met and walked in the hall and downstairs, conversing, even though the judge admonished witnesses not to talk to other witnesses.

Something else that didn't seem right involved the jury. Members had been instructed not to discuss the case or any subject involved in it. Yet my attorney's wife once overheard two jurors discussing the case in the elevator.

It now seems clear that the man in the truck was not the attacker, but the victim believed he was her assailant and the prosecuting attorney made a big deal about the truck. That truck's similarity to one owned by Rick's company first linked me to the crime in the course of the investigation. The connection was circumstantial, but even I must admit it was damning.

Many other people testified, including the two policemen who were first at the crime scene and responded to the victim's home. At the crime scene, they had found the disc from Allison's CD player and her flip-flops and returned them to her.

My jaw dropped when I heard this. I wanted to scream, "That CD could have had the man's fingerprints on it!" For some unknown reason, the CD could no longer be located.

The deputy probation officer who searched for me after I ran from work furlough also testified. He participated in the search of my storage unit and said that when the authorities located my pickup at the airport (where I'd left it when I flew to Texas), they found inside it a print-out about me from the sheriff's fugitive website. The man hadn't mentioned this in his earlier report, however, and authorities didn't collect the picture for evidence.

Rage at this falsehood filled me, and I practically flew out of my chair. How could he say such a thing? I told my attorneys they needed to locate that picture and test it for fingerprints, because if a print-out actually had been found in my truck, then it must have been planted. I had no such picture in my possession, ever. That fact didn't matter. The supposed print-out gave the impression I had knowledge of being a suspect and therefore fled the state.

The man also testified to finding a police scanner in my pickup, which was true. Being naturally curious and somewhat paranoid about the cops, I occasionally listened to nearby law enforcement communications. The fact that I owned a scanner added to investigators' assumptions that I was guilty, and I'm sure increased my guilt in the minds of the jurors.

Throughout my trial, the detective caused my greatest anger. I feel no ill-will toward the man now (although I do believe he should be held accountable for his deceptions), but then I viewed him as my nemesis. In addition to botching the photo lineup, he'd presented a misleading version of events when he testified at my preliminary hearing. I had despised him then, and the way he embellished his account at the trial fueled my anger like pouring gas on an open flame.

When my attorney questioned him about the photo lineup, he admitted that the victim had said she was having a hard time recognizing her assailant. The detective conjectured about a small abrasion on my forehead in the work furlough booking photo. That open sore, caused by my meth use, led to speculation that it may have been an injury from when the victim hit her attacker with her CD player. My attorney cross-examined the detective extensively about changes he made to the artist sketch composites without even showing the victim. He changed his story numerous times and testified about certain facts of his investigation that were contrary to his own notes.

Others in the courtroom—perhaps even members of the jury—realized his inconsistencies and deceptions, but none of it mattered because the victim believed me to be her attacker.

One witness I appreciated was Dr. Ralph Norman Haber, who has a PhD in experimental psychology and was an expert on eyewitness identification. Because this was a case of mistaken identity, he was hired to testify in my defense. The DA tried desperately to keep him from testifying, stating it would be unfair and prejudicial. In the end, the judge allowed it, but the good doctor was frequently abused and disrespected. I was shocked at how contemptuously both the state and the court treated a man who simply offered his expertise on matters most people are ignorant about. He had no ulterior motives or agenda, except to speak about certain facts and what studies have proven in regard to eyewitness IDs.

Haber related that victims have a harder time identifying their attackers than bystanders because of the stress they endure during the assault. He said high levels of stress can actually impede an eyewitness's ability to perceive and that "post-event information" (such as viewing a photograph of a suspect) can even modify a witness's memory. He shared his opinion that the photo lineup was unfair because the background of my photo was a different color than the others and that I was the only person with light brown hair. Haber said when someone is shown multiple lineups, it reduces the reliability of the ultimate identification.

Other people testified before and after this point: post office employees, other law enforcement, investigators for the DA and the defense, the doctor who performed the rape exam, and more.

My fellow employee testified that we worked side by side and he could see me throughout our shift on November 24. He said he left for about twenty minutes to grab lunch, but I was there before he left and when he returned. He also testified that he did not observe any cuts or abrasions on my face that day.

The court called the next witness. "Rick Gambino."

My heart raced. Rick's testimony was my best hope for a not-guilty verdict. After he was sworn in, he took his seat, and my attorney asked him a series of questions, establishing the length of his relationship with me and my mom.

Rick testified that I did not live with him and Mom at the time of the crime. When asked how many times their house was raided after I ran from work furlough, he said, "I would say at least six, if not eight times."

"What times of day?"

"All times of day. We had one incident at midnight where a dog and uniformed officers fully armed came into our home. And, you know, we always opened our doors up wide to anybody. We always told them. 'Uriah Courtney doesn't live here.'"

Rick also testified that I was not allowed to use the white Nissan truck. He didn't even permit me to have the keys, because I had been involved in an accident that caused some minor damage to it.

When the DA cross-examined Rick, I was so proud of him. Despite her obvious ire and apparent presumption that he was covering for his stepson, Rick remained calm and articulate. The DA repeatedly prefaced questions with "when the detective came to your home to interview you" and Rick consistently responded that the detective had never been to his home.

"I've never even seen the detective. I only spoke to him on the phone." Rick waved slightly and glanced at the audience. "If the detective was in the courtroom right now, I wouldn't even know him." (The detective was there, but Rick didn't know it.)

Eventually, the DA stomped her foot, walked back to the table, and threw down her papers. "No more questions, your honor!"

I guess I hoped for a great hammer blow to the prosecution, testimony so powerful and convincing it would sweep away all the lies and deceit like a tidal wave. That didn't happen.

USPS employees testified that I looked like one of the contractors and I was never absent from work during the week of Thanksgiving 2004. A payroll clerk identified my paycheck issued on December 3, 2004, for the work period which included November 24. A purchasing specialist identified a pay voucher requesting pay for Courtney for eight hours on November 24.

In essence, those who believed in my guilt must have thought all these people conspired to cover up my crime.

Every morning of my trial, I followed the same routine: early morning rising, going through the series of holding cells, and waiting in my borrowed suit. I prayed and recited psalms, especially reflecting on each verse of Psalm 23. I read a few pages from my hidden pocket Bible and prayed some more.

Every time the bailiff did a pat-down, he discovered my pocket Bible in my sock. And each time, he stuck it back.

He and I had a pretty long walk from the holding cell to the courtroom and not once did I sense any animosity from him. He heard every minute of testimony from every person at my trial. He also heard all the legal wrangling among my attorneys, the DA, and the judge. I often wondered what he believed regarding my guilt or innocence.

My mom was invariably the first one in the courtroom each day. I always turned around to look at her and either whispered or spoke out loud, "I love you, Mom." Seeing her comforted my soul. But I also grieved that she was exposed to my public disgrace. I could imagine what the jurors and observers thought of her: the wretched mother of this perverted sexual predator. Day after day, she sat silently listening to my accusers and maligners. Later I learned how the mother of the victim glared at her so malevolently each day that she felt physically threatened.

Other family and friends, including Jessica, were present during my trial. Dad attended just one morning. When he and other family members met for lunch, he expressed his anger about this injustice in such a violent manner that my family decided it would be better if he did not return to the courtroom. After that, he agonized from afar.

Every day during the noon recess, I sat in a dim little holding cell directly behind the courtroom. My lunch always consisted of a small carton of juice, some mystery meat, a soggy cookie, and a peanut butter and jelly sandwich.

One day during my trial, I remained confined there for three hours. I was told the judge and the DA had left to attend an awards ceremony together, and the usual lunch break was extended to accommodate their presence at this event. I already felt I wasn't receiving a fair trial based on what I'd observed of the antagonism between them and my attorney, but the thought of the DA and the judge going off together to some quasi-social event in the middle of my trial nearly pushed me over the edge.

I paced the tiny cell while my anger burned white hot.

As the trial dragged on, the misrepresentations became more difficult to take. I could hardly keep quiet during this charade. On an almost daily basis, I wanted to jump out of my seat and yell, "Why can't anyone else see that this is all a lie?" The victim and eyewitness could have been honestly mistaken, but I felt the others were distorting facts and fabricating a story to fit circumstantial evidence and the many coincidences.

Most days, upon returning to my cell, I felt utterly defeated. With Psalm 10:1, my spirit cried, "Why, O Lord, do you stand far away? Why do you hide yourself in times of trouble?" God's silence made no sense to me. Feeling forsaken and all alone, I wondered why he wasn't causing the trial to go in my favor. Pain and perplexity produced all kinds of questions, yet the Lord remained silent. When I was suffering such isolation and humiliation, daily facing jury members who no doubt were disgusted at the sight of me, death seemed the only solution.

At one point, I got so low that I planned to sneak in a razor blade. The minute the deputy turned, I would jump out of my seat and leap onto the desk of the DA, cut my wrist and neck and bleed out on top of her, yelling, "My blood is on your hands!"

The idea crystallized in my mind, but then the indwelling Holy Spirit struck a mighty blow to my conscience and shattered the scheme to pieces. How could I do such a thing to my mom or to my son? How could I do such a thing to Christ? We had been in deep communion all this time. Would I give up and let the enemy prevail?

Thinking back on those days not long after they had passed, I realized something I didn't know then: I actually felt closer to God than I had ever before experienced. There was nothing like it and nothing I can compare it to now. He comforted me through the beautiful words in the Psalms and by the power of the Holy Spirit, enabling me to apply those texts to my experience. Could I have endured such a trial by my own strength? No, I wanted to die. But the Lord wrapped me up with his Spirit and protected me from myself, from others, and the devil. If it weren't so, I wouldn't be here today, alive and well in Christ.

Toward the end of my trial, an officer testified about the search of my storage unit. He had nothing to say of any value to the case, and I wondered why the DA put him on the stand. She questioned him about a few things the jury had already heard. But as he answered her questions, he subtly dropped the bombshell I felt would finish me off. He said they also discovered "guns" in my storage unit.

My attorney leapt to his feet. For once, the judge sustained his objection and then admonished the jury to disregard the statement. But it was too late. I was sure they would want to rid the streets of me after all they had heard. In their minds, I was an accused rapist, kidnapper, big-time drug dealer, and now one in possession of firearms. Who would want a person like that in society, in our community, and around our children? *Away with him, for he is not fit to be free!*

This information was disclosed on the eve of closing arguments, and my attorney requested a mistrial. The judge rejected his request, stating that

I could take it up on appeal if I got convicted (something he said a number of times throughout my trial).

Because the State has the burden of proof in showing why the defendant is guilty and should be convicted, the DA went first with closing arguments. They were lengthy and dramatic. "Use your common sense, ladies and gentlemen. Look at the totality of evidence and you will find only one reasonable conclusion, that the defendant is guilty of all the crimes alleged against him. Send a message to this defendant that his actions will not be tolerated in our society. This is not a case of mistaken identity. Not a case of an alibi. There is no alibi." She went on to say a great deal about the truck, claiming it was evidence against me.

In my attorney's closing arguments, he stated that the DA's case was based on a series of wrong assumptions. "We have a truck that is not even available to Mr. Courtney on the day of the incident. That's all. That's the prosecution's entire case against Mr. Courtney. He wasn't allowed to drive the truck, he didn't have access to it, he didn't have keys to it." He continued, "Uriah didn't even have the opportunity to commit the crime. This is a crime of opportunity. Think about it. The prosecution would have you believe Mr. Courtney left the Midway Post Office, or he just didn't show up that day, even though people said he did. He drove out to Ocean Beach [where Mom and Rick lived], switched out trucks, drove all the way out to Lemon Grove . . . committed the attack, and got back to work without anybody ever noticing."

He concluded that the case was not about sending messages, it was about determining if the prosecution proved its case against Mr. Courtney. "Please do not speculate. Please do not guess. Don't become one of those juries that convict an innocent man based on wrongful, mistaken, inaccurate testimony. Don't convict an innocent man just because the guilty man is still out there." He said it would take real courage for the jurors to tell the detective, "You got the wrong guy." But that's what they had to say in their verdict.

In the DA's rebuttal, she refuted everything my attorney had just said. Then she quoted the victim, "This is something I am never going to forget."

I sat in my awkward suit and thought how that statement would resonate with the jury. Who wouldn't feel sorry for the young woman? Who wouldn't want to believe that her identification was accurate?

Then the DA said, "Ladies and gentlemen, the defendant got a fair trial in this case. I told you at the beginning, this case was about truth, this case is about justice. And if justice isn't for everyone, then really justice isn't for anyone. And Allison is entitled to justice. And the only justice in this case is to find the defendant guilty."

The judge thanked the members of the jury and gave them further instructions before dismissing them.

While they deliberated, I sat in the little holding cell behind the courtroom. The room was secluded, and I felt alone and afraid. I knew that focusing on fear and worry indicated a lack of trust in God. If God is all-knowing, all-wise, and all-powerful, why fret so much? I told myself to trust him and believe he would deliver me from my accusers and restore my freedom. Bits of Scripture flitted through my head: *Why are you cast down, O my soul, and why are you in turmoil within me? Hope in God. Do not be anxious about anything, but in everything by prayer and supplication with thanksgiving let your requests be made known to God. And the peace of God, which surpasses all understanding, will guard your hearts and minds in Christ Jesus. For to this you have been called, because Christ also suffered for you, leaving you an example, so that you might follow in his steps.*

But I didn't want to suffer anymore. I wanted this "fiery trial" to end.

The verdict was returned in less than twenty-four hours, at 9:00 a.m. on Thursday, March 16, 2006. I willed myself to stay calm, to not let my heart be troubled, but it was impossible. I had endured this torture with the hope for coming relief and remained hopeful even now, but my mental anguish caused my heart to physically ache.

The jurors entered the courtroom and passed by me one by one. I looked at each face, longing to see some positive sign, perhaps a smile or a nod. But I saw only their profiles as they looked toward the judge's bench.

The judge spoke to the jury: "It is my understanding the jury has reached a verdict. You came back yesterday around 11:30 a.m. and the forms were sealed by direction of the court because I couldn't get counsel here before noon, and I was leaving at noon to attend a funeral."

Yes. I had waited the rest of the day and the entire night—all those extra hours after the jury had made its decision—in suspense.

The judge asked the foreperson to review the forms to make sure they were as presented to the court on the previous day. After that was confirmed, a deputy took the forms and handed them to the judge. The judge asked me to stand and face the jury box.

My heart raced so wildly I thought I might die right then from cardiac arrest. My knees shook and my legs felt like wet noodles. Doing my best to keep myself from falling over, I waited to hear the verdict read aloud. The proceedings had the appearance of justice at work, but I felt it was all a façade. Nevertheless, I willed myself to believe the jury was about to set things right.

The judge read, "In the Superior Court of the State of California, in and for the County of San Diego, we, the jury in the above-entitled case, find the defendant, Uriah Courtney, guilty of the crime of kidnap, carry away to commit sexual penetration." My mouth went completely dry, and my chin hit my chest. I grabbed the edge of the table to stay on my feet. Agonized cries broke out behind me from a bereaved mother, a devastated fianceé, a bewildered stepfather, a grief-stricken brother, and a heartbroken sister.

More charges were read. "Same court, guilty of the crime of rape by foreign object, use of force. Same court, guilty of the crime of false imprisonment." Each guilty verdict smashed into me like a wrecking ball.

It was all over now. I had been found guilty. I desperately needed to hug my mom. I knew she was grieving immensely and I just wanted to convey and feel the comfort that can be derived only from physical touch. But it wasn't allowed. All I could do was turn and say, "I love you," as I was led from the courtroom.

13

Post-Trial Despair

San Diego County Jail, 6th Floor

I hung up the phone. Once again, Jessica had not answered my call.

Stumbling blindly back to my cell, my mind filled with pleas to God. *Haven't I suffered enough, Lord? I've lost everything. Why won't you bring these trials and tribulations to an end? Please stop the pain.*

Ever since my trial had ended, Jessica had been distant and cold. I knew she was suffering in her own way, frightened about living in a new city while working and raising our son. But I felt a distressing situation should push a couple closer together, not further apart. I was already a broken man, devastated beyond words, and this emotional desertion felt like a stake driven into the heart of our relationship.

All this time, I'd been thinking things would work out for us—if I could only get out of jail. I'd prayed fervently for the Lord to strengthen our relationship by bringing this calamity to a screeching halt. I also prayed that I would be able to raise my son in the Lord. I agonized over the thought of not being there for him. I wanted to hug him, play with him, watch him grow, and tuck him into bed at night. I wanted to be his daddy not through a thick glass, but in truth, in reality, in presence.

Then my mom and sister had visited me and shared distressing information about seeing Jessica with another man. Convinced I could not bear another frowning providence, I had begged the Lord over and over again to make the pain go away.

After two days and nights of agonizing heartache and sleeplessness, I felt relief as sweet as a cool ocean breeze on a hot summer day. I still grieved, but the Lord filled my spirit with his peace.

A little later, Jessica came to see me. It warmed my heart to see Colton with her. My precious son looked so handsome. I longed to break the glass to embrace him, to protect him from the confusion I was sure he would soon experience. Jessica and I began speaking, and I tried to remain calm as I asked her why she had deserted me.

She told me she was scared and alone and couldn't do things any more on her own. "You might be going away for life. What am I supposed to do? I'm almost a 40-year-old woman, and I don't want be alone anymore. I still love you and want to be with you, but I just can't wait any longer."

For a minute, I let it all sink in, trying to process what she'd said and come up with a reasonable response.

"I actually understand your feelings of loneliness, because I'm lonely, too." I blinked. "I can't blame you for wanting to move on, because nobody knows when I'll get out, but couldn't you have at least waited until after I find out whether or not I'll get a retrial?"

The conversation continued a few minutes longer, deteriorating badly. My parting words were, "Watch what kind of trash you bring around my son."

We both stood. Jessica picked up Colton, turned around, and walked out. That was the last glimpse I had of him for more than seven years.

*

Remember the judge's frequent assurance that I could appeal my conviction? It didn't take me long to begin working on that. But my family and I decided we needed a new attorney. On April 18, 2006, Jonathan Jordan filed a motion for a new trial based on juror misconduct, verdict contrary to evidence, newly discovered evidence, ineffective assistance of counsel, and miscarriage of justice.

He'd told me a new trial was a long shot, but we'd give it our best effort. Meanwhile, I remained in the same cell on the sixth floor. Cellies came and went in a stream that drifted out of memory. My son and his mother moved away. I descended into a chasm of hopelessness.

And then the trial judge rejected my appeal motion.

My privileges were revoked, and I was no longer permitted to attend educational classes. By then, I think I'd lost the ability to be more distressed than I already was. Losing that little bit of liberty was nothing compared to my other losses.

My sentencing date was June 1, 2007.

I entered the courtroom with my shackles on as usual, but wearing my jail house attire, as my appearance no longer mattered. Like my entire trial, the suit had been just a pretense. Despite feeling defeated, I tried to hold my head high. Allison wasn't in the courtroom, but her mother was, as well as another woman who read a statement by the victim. The mother's contempt for me was palpable, and I couldn't blame her. She stared at the man she and her daughter believed committed this unforgivable act of violence, ruining the girl's life and stealing her innocence.

After the other woman read the victim's letter, I was given opportunity to address the court. I had hoped and prayed Allison would be there to hear my voice for the first time and perhaps realize her mistake. I read this letter:

> First of all, I'd like to thank God for giving me the strength to persevere through this nightmare. Second, I want to thank each and every one of my family members and loved ones for all their love and support, especially you, Mom. I love and miss you all very much.
>
> Your Honor, since I have been convicted of this crime I imagine the court would like to see me show some kind of remorse, but how can one show remorse for something he didn't do? I am an innocent man who's been wrongfully accused and convicted of a crime I did not and would not ever commit. People who commit crimes of this nature are mentally sick, and that is a sickness that is in no way a part of me. I have morals, compassion, and regard for other human beings. Going out and destroying someone else's life—someone's innocence—is not something I would do. And now, because it is I who have been convicted of this crime, Allison's real attacker is still out there. Every time I read an article in the newspaper about another woman who has been attacked, it makes me feel so sad and depressed, because I can't help but wonder if it's the same man who attacked Allison, and is the cause of all of this.
>
> Allison, my thoughts and prayers go out to you, and I wish you the best in the process of healing. No one should ever have to experience the defiling and degradation of one's body like you did. I can't even imagine the horror, hurt, and pain you must have felt and are still going through. This was an act of complete disregard to your mind, body, and soul, and I feel so very sorry for you. I know you probably hate me and justifiably so, but your hatred is

directed at the wrong person. I'm sorry, Allison, but you are mistaken in your identification of me as your attacker. It was a simple mistake, but one that has had monumental repercussions, because now neither one of us is receiving the justice we deserve. I hope and pray for the both of us that the man who actually attacked you is captured and brought to justice so he can't hurt anyone else, and so we both can have peace and the justice we seek.

If I'd had proper representation from the beginning of this case, I believe the truth would have been more thoroughly searched out and established in order to prove that I did not commit this crime. I was mistaken for having [my initial attorneys] handle this case. They were totally incompetent and completely unprepared for my trial. They didn't work together as a team, and [my attorney's] conduct before and throughout my trial was absolutely unacceptable. I wish now that I had fired them before my trial even began, but I didn't know the options available to me, my rights, or what to do once things had already been set in motion. I just thought that because I was innocent I would receive justice. Your Honor, Allison and her family are undeniably the true victims in this case, but they are not the only ones whose lives have been so utterly devastated by the actions of another man. My family and I have become his victims too, by being dragged into this nightmare. So, I ask that you would please take these things into consideration and have mercy on an innocent man.

After reading my statement, I sat down. Rick read a letter describing the role of memory in recalling the past and stating that my conviction prevented me, the victim, and the perpetrator from receiving justice. The judge addressed the attorneys on some legal issues. Then I was asked to stand while the judge sentenced me. I stared at the judge, not malevolently, just waiting for him to inflict the final sword thrust.

He spoke: "Mr. Courtney, in the interest of justice, this court sentences you to a term of life with the possibility of parole, plus eight years, eight months."

If I could have cried, I might have. But like so many things, the release of tears had long since deserted me.

The eight years and eight months represented the maximum possible time on the drug charges for which I'd already been sentenced to work furlough and charges connected to items found in my storage unit.

Ten days later on June 11, 2007, which I did not know was the day before I would be sent to prison, I wrote this letter to my mother:

Dear Mom,

No matter how long it takes until I'm able to write to you again, please try to keep your worries to a minimum. I know that's easier said than done because I have a hard time doing it myself, but I believe God would not allow me to be sent to prison if he weren't going to protect me while I'm there. He's protected me throughout my entire reckless life, and I've no doubt he will continue to do so now. Always remember that this is only temporary, just like everything else in this world. God has his reasons for allowing this to happen. I can't say that I like it, but I do have to accept it for what it is and do the best I can. Who knows what God is going to do with me while I'm in prison? Maybe he's going to make me an even better and stronger man. I'm going to try and find a way to channel my anger into something positive and productive. Hopefully, it will be helping others to come to know the Lord. I feel like that is something he wants me to do. Anyway, I know God will prepare me for whatever he wants me to do. All right, Mom, I love you soooo much.

Love, your son,
Uriah

Despite my emotional descent, I spent more time in prayer and Bible reading. I needed spiritual strength, biblical knowledge, and the Spirit's comfort. Even with God's equipping power, I would barely stand under the unjust punishment the devil's world system was about to bring down upon my head.

14

Solitary Confinement

Richard J. Donovan Correctional Facility

A voice boomed from the call box in my cell: "Uriah Courtney, wake up and prepare to be transferred."

My heart pounded. I'd known I would be shipped off to prison soon, but for security reasons inmates aren't told the exact date. Now I knew: June 12, 2007. As I picked up my meager possessions (Bible, stamps, envelopes), anxiety flooded me like a tsunami.

Deputies brought the inmates being transferred down to the second floor. They confined us in holding tanks, prepared paperwork, and took inventory of our property.

One by one, we were removed from the cell and lined up against the wall where the sheriff's deputies put our shackles on, chaining us two by two. From the jail, it was only a short ride—maybe twenty-five minutes—to the R. J. Donovan Correctional Facility, which sits southeast of San Diego, in the Otay Mesa area near the Mexican border. My heart ached as the bus drove past the turnoff that led to my parents' house in Imperial Beach.

When we drew near the prison, I saw the sun reflecting off glass in the guard towers and razor wire atop the high chain link fences. Actually, fences within fences. My heart hammered even harder, and I wondered if the guy beside me could sense my growing fear. Our bus entered the prison grounds and rolled to a stop behind a large cinder block building. We were told to stay seated.

The officers led a few of us at a time into the building, which was called R & R, for Receiving and Release. Inside, a number of Correctional Officers (COs) stood in a line, wearing latex gloves. They told us to strip down, lift our genitals, bend over, and cough.

Once that was finished, they gave each of us a bright orange prison outfit, similar to the county jail clothing but a different color. Then they put us inside holding cells.

Never before had I been in such an overcrowded cell. So many inmates were shoved inside it was standing room only. Being confined to such a small space was bad enough, but this was horrible. The pressure and stench overpowered me.

I recognized a few faces, but I didn't know their names. Did any of them know what I was in for? If so, they probably wouldn't do anything now, but would wait until they saw me on the prison yard. What violence might they use then?

The thought of going into protective custody or the prison's Sensitive Needs Yard (SNY) flitted through my mind, but I immediately dismissed it. I'd heard horror stories about SNY, and I had no desire to be confined with a bunch of rapists and child molesters. No, I'd do this time on my own terms, and if that meant taking a huge personal risk by staying in general population, then so be it.

Hours later, my name was finally called. A CO led me into the captain's office. Panic skyrocketed. Why was he bringing me here, when everyone else was being processed up front?

A sergeant and another CO stood in the captain's office. The captain glanced up. "Take a seat."

I sat in front of his desk while he perused my paperwork. After a minute or so, he looked at me. "Do you have any safety concerns? If so, would you like to go to the Sensitive Needs Yard?"

I promptly answered, "No. And No."

He asked about my charges, convictions, and the items found in my storage unit. I wasn't sure where this conversation was going, so I asked, "What's the purpose of all these questions?"

"You're a ward of the state now. And you're a high-risk inmate due to the seriousness of your charges. Are you certain you don't have any safety concerns?"

"I'm sure."

He then had me sign some papers and dismissed me. The CO escorted me to another holding cell. This one wasn't nearly as crowded and I could sit on the floor with my back against the wall.

I thought about what had just happened and wondered if I'd made the right decision to stay in GP (General Population). Prison would be no different from county jail. If anything, inmates could be even more vicious. What was I going to do? My mind raced, and I felt like everyone was staring at me.

In fact, as I looked around the musty-smelling room, I saw fear on other men's faces. Most spoke animatedly with the inmate next to them about past prison experiences, but a few appeared visibly afraid. That realization comforted me.

By now, it was late afternoon. I was taken from the holding tank and placed in a long line of other inmates. We were told to keep quiet and led in single file to a different building. After about an hour in another holding tank, I was brought to a psych doctor's office. He asked a series of questions, one of which was, "Are you feeling suicidal or homicidal at this time?"

That's it. I'd found a way to use the system to my advantage.

I replied, "Yes, I am suicidal. I've just been sentenced to life in prison and I don't want to live anymore."

The doctor called out to the CO standing in the hallway, "This inmate needs to be taken to the crisis unit."

The CO strode into the room. "Stand up."

I stood, and he handcuffed me. He led me out of the room and put me inside a cell alone. A few minutes later, he returned and escorted me back over to R & R.

There he put me inside a literal cage. Constructed of heavy-duty angle iron and rigid steel mesh, it was around six feet tall and only about two and a half feet square.

He said, "Turn around." He opened a small door on the cage. "Stick your hands through this opening so I can remove the handcuffs."

I complied.

Then he said, "Take off all your clothes and hand them to me."

Again I obeyed.

He took them and disappeared.

I scrunched down on the cold floor of the cage with my knees to my chest, naked and humiliated.

A few minutes later, he came back with a pair of boxer briefs, which he shoved through the slot. "Put these on."

I slipped on the briefs and the CO disappeared again. I'm not sure how long I sat, shivering on the floor of that tiny cage with my arms wrapped around my knees, wondering what they would do to me next.

*

My construction experience enabled me to estimate length fairly accurately, and I believe those steel screen sides were no more than thirty-two inches wide. By the time I was placed in that cage, it was late in the evening.

Perhaps an hour later, a CO came over and told me to stand up, turn around, and put my hand through the little opening. Handcuffed once again behind the back, I was taken outside and conducted across the main plaza of the prison to the crisis unit.

Darkness had descended, and I looked up at the star-filled sky. I couldn't remember the last time I'd seen stars. Their pinpoints glittered in the dark desert night. I caught my breath. Despite my mental numbness, the beauty of the night pierced my soul and generated praise to God.

All too soon, the CO lifted a key hooked to a loop on his belt and unlocked a heavy steel door before us. We walked down a short corridor with cells on each side.

The CO brought me into a room where a nurse stood. She asked me a variety of questions. Then she said, "I'm going to inject you with Haldol."

The size of the syringe's barrel, filled with gold-colored liquid, shocked me. The dose seemed enough for a horse. It burned a bit when she shot it into my shoulder. She rubbed a cotton ball over the injection site. "This will help you sleep, and tomorrow you'll see the doctor."

Wearing only a heavy and uncomfortable smock, I was placed inside an extremely cold cell. A thin blue plastic mat lay on the floor in the corner. The CO handed me a blanket made of the same material as my smock. It reminded me of something you might find inside a moving van. He said this type of material prevented me from shredding it and using it to hurt myself.

I reclined on the mat and pulled the heavy blanket over my head. For some time, I lay still and let my mind wander. I was in prison now. For the rest of my life. How terrifying!

The drug eventually took effect. The next thing I remember is waking to a very loud and annoying tap, tap, tap. I heard a voice. I thought I was dreaming, but the sounds continued. When my mind fog cleared, I realized a CO was tapping his large key against the door of my cell.

"You want to eat some breakfast?"

Still groggy, I struggled to my feet and stumbled to the door. The little flap in the middle of it clanged open, and a tray slid inside. I grabbed it and quickly returned to my mat, where I scarfed down the food. I don't recall eating anything the day before.

When I finished, I put the tray on the floor in front of the door and lay back down. I was restless and very cold.

Sometime later, the door opened. A CO walked in with a doctor. The doctor asked many questions, which I answered as best I could. At this point, I really didn't care about answering correctly or even truthfully. All I could think about was the cold.

At the first opportunity, I told him, "I'm freezing and I want some real clothes—at least some socks and underwear."

"If you promise not to hurt yourself, I'll get you some clothes."

"I promise."

He asked what types of medications I'd been taking, and I told him I was on an antidepressant. Not satisfied with only that, he prescribed other medications as well. After all, I was suicidal.

A short time after they left, a CO came to the door with a female nurse. The CO gave me a pair of socks, boxer briefs, and a T-shirt. How happy I was to have these items! I immediately dropped the smock to the floor and put everything on.

The nurse handed the smock to the CO and gave me a paper cup full of pills, which I swallowed down with some water. She politely asked me to stick out my tongue to ensure that I had swallowed everything.

They left, and I returned to lie on my mat. The pills were supposed to help me relax, even sleep, but I couldn't. My mind whirled. I felt like I was going crazy and must do something. I needed to read. Reading had become my new addiction, but I didn't have a single book in my possession.

I pounded on my cell door.

After a few minutes, a CO came over. "What do you want?"

"Can I get a Bible? Or at least a book?"

"That's up to your doctor. You'll have to ask him when he comes back tomorrow."

The next day—and another deal between the good doc and myself—he informed the CO that I was now allowed to have reading material and could even write to my family. I was led out into the hallway where a large bookshelf stood, filled with books.

This may sound sacrilegious, but I felt as if I'd gone to heaven. Not only did I discover a Bible, but also many novels from some favorite authors. I was permitted to take two novels plus the Bible. It was like Christmas, and I rushed back to my cell to open my presents.

First I said a prayer and read the Bible. The Psalms had always encouraged me, and they comforted me as I read them now. Once I finished this devotional time, I began reading one of the novels.

A guy about my age occupied the cell next to mine, and we talked to each other through the air vent. He certainly was an entertaining fellow. Apparently he was there because he had stuck a paperclip inside his penis. Whatever his reasons, this wasn't the first time he'd done that.

We enjoyed a lot of the same music, so when bored we'd sing together as loudly as possible. Sometimes a CO told us to quiet down, but we were entertaining ourselves, and the CO's ire only added to our amusement.

During this time, a correctional counselor came to discuss my points, which dictated that I would be going to a Level 4 yard. In California, that's usually maximum security. She explained that because Donovan's only Level 4 yard was SNY I would be transferred to another prison once I got endorsed, which could take up to three months. She also told me Nevada had a felony warrant out for my arrest.

I literally scoffed at that. I had just been sentenced to life in prison in California and now Nevada wanted a piece of my hide? *Well, they're just going to have to wait their turn*, I thought. *What a cruel joke!* Much later, Nevada would seem to have the last laugh.

Once a week, I wrote to my parents, telling them how my conviction had discouraged and depressed me. This attitude wreaked havoc on my mental state and my relationship with God. Gradually an unsettled acceptance began to seep into my mind, although I continually reaffirmed my belief that God would someday cause me to be exonerated.

My parents knew I was in the crisis unit but didn't know exactly why. I carefully worded my letters to avoid inflicting additional worries on Mom's already grief-stricken heart.

Was I really suicidal? No. Did I sometimes want to die? Absolutely. When I could no longer bear my burden, I prayed for God to take my life.

Meanwhile I attempted to manipulate the system like Jacob (Gen 30:25–43), in an effort to avoid SNY and get endorsed to a soft yard, where they housed inmates with psych issues and no one would care about your paperwork. But the Lord thwarted my attempt to control my own destiny.

The doctor knew I was malingering and wanted to put a stop to it. He had previously worked on the SNY reception yard and told me numerous times that it wasn't nearly as bad as I thought. But he couldn't convince me.

After about a month and a half, a sergeant and the doctor paid me a visit. The sergeant said, "Uriah, you're going to be made SNY, and you'll be leaving the crisis unit today."

I did not take this news lightly. I began yelling at him and the doctor. "I refuse to go! If you try taking me, I'll just kill myself!"

The sergeant calmly responded, "We will take you by force, if necessary. Once you get to Ad-Seg, we'll take your clothes and your books and keep you on suicide watch."

The thought of losing my precious books convinced me to cooperate. I signed the paperwork and off I went to Ad-Seg (Administrative Segregation, aka "the hole").

The following day, I wrote to my parents: "I feel as if I've entered through the gates of hell and into Satan's warehouse of human souls."

The hole was my introduction to actually being in prison. The CO led me—handcuffed and wearing only boxer shorts and T-shirt—through the U-shaped building with two tiers of cells. Some inmates looked out through the small glass windows of their cells. Others stared at me from the same little cages as I'd been confined to earlier. In Ad-Seg, no one wears a regular prison outfit, only white boxers and a T-shirt.

My cell was a third of the size of my last one, but it had a thicker mattress, a small metal table attached to the wall, and a window—an actual window—through which I could look outside.

Every day, I'd sit in front of that window for hours, reading or writing letters or poems. On many occasions, I watched black crows and red-tailed hawks soar in the blue sky. Jackrabbits hopped around in the dusk, sometimes making me smile with their entertaining antics. What enthralling scenes for my starved senses!

A week or two after I'd arrived in Ad-Seg, I appeared before the review board to be informed that I would go to the SNY yard. It was the same one I was already on, but I'd move from Building 7 to Building 9.

When I returned to my cell, excitement and fear vied for first place in my mind. After two months of solitary confinement, the prospect of walking outside on the yard and meeting other people thrilled me. Maybe I'd even meet brothers in Christ. And I couldn't wait to see Mom and Rick again. But I was scared. SNY or not, prison politics would still exist. And it wouldn't take much for my cover to be blown—like the wrong cellie. If he asked to see my paperwork, and I refused, he would automatically assume I was in for some type of sexual offense. Word would spread, and I'd be forever tormented.

That evening I was moved. A CO came to my door, cuffed me, and walked me out of hell's gates. Outside the building, he stopped and removed the handcuffs. Then he handed me an orange prison outfit, exactly like the one I'd been given two months earlier but lost due to my self-determined detour. I hurriedly donned it, and the CO escorted me about a hundred yards to Building 9, where I'd meet the first—and worst—of my many prison cellies.

15

Lengthy Limbo

Richard J. Donovan Correctional Facility, Reception

The door to cell 116 slid open. Inside stood a wiry, tatted guy. Swastikas covered his arms, head, and torso. A large tattoo on his back depicted a crucified skinhead.

My heart sank.

He turned toward me. "Name's Sick."

"Uriah." I hoped my voice didn't convey my dread. Our brief initial conversation consisted of some meaningless prison talk, but later he identified himself as a skinhead dropout. Then he said, "That's why I'm in SNY. Why are you here?"

"I got a life sentence for a crime I didn't commit. You know how it is for young white boys. I didn't want to get caught up in a gang and forced to participate in all their drama."

"So how'd you get a life sentence?"

"Convicted for kidnapping and robbery."

He grunted and sat on his bunk, where he picked up a book.

I'd have the upper rack, which was okay by me. And if he spent most of his time reading, we might get along better than I thought.

My appeal to the State Appellate Court generated legal mail, which is distributed differently than regular mail. Floor officers deliver most mail, but a different CO goes to all the buildings and calls you to the cell door to sign for and receive your legal letters.

A few days after my arrival in Building 9, this CO came to our cell door. "Courtney. Legal mail."

Sick stared at me. "What's that all about?"

"Oh, it's just from the appellate attorney handling my appeal to the State Board."

"You're appealing the kidnapping and robbery conviction?"

"Yeah." I sat on my rack.

Sick stood. "So how did that go down?"

"A teenaged boy was walking along a street and someone robbed him. I was accused and wrongfully convicted of it."

He nodded. "Same thing happened to a buddy of mine. He was in the wrong place at the wrong time."

People who heard about my case often assumed that, but I wanted to set the record straight. "It wasn't like that. I was actually at work when the crime occurred."

He shrugged as if he didn't believe me. After that, things quickly soured between us. Small conflicts often led to serious words.

Some time later, he got upset and sucker-punched me in the jaw. Earlier in my life, I would have reacted with violence. But I merely sat back on my bunk and picked up the book that had flown out of my hands. I wasn't going to give him a fight unless I absolutely had to. If I complained to the COs about him, I'd be labeled a snitch. Other skinhead dropouts admired Sick, and even the COs treated him with deference.

For two weeks, I asked if I could be moved. But the COs kept telling me I had to wait until they did convenience moves. Finally I'd had enough.

While our section of the tier was served breakfast one morning, instead of returning to eat in my cell, I set my tray on the table in the dayroom and just stood there.

The next section can't be released until all inmates are back in their cells, so two stocky COs confronted me.

One got in my face. "What's your problem, Courtney?"

I gripped the edge of the metal table. "I'm suicidal."

He snorted and the other shook his head. They grabbed me by the arms and dragged me over to the open cell door. As they tried forcing me through, I lifted my feet and braced one against each side of the doorway.

That really ticked them off. They each grabbed an arm and a leg and tossed me inside the cell, quickly signaling for the tower to slide the door shut behind me.

Inside the cell, Sick stood with crossed arms and a menacing smile. I walked past him—expecting to get punched and have to fight for my life—and sat on my bunk. About an hour later, a CO came to the door, put me in cuffs, and escorted me over to CTC (the crisis unit). I received another huge shot of Haldol and was put inside an ice-cold room, wearing nothing but a smock. I remained shivering there for four long days.

*

That was my last time in CTC. It was also the last time I had any physical altercation with a cellie. Even though I didn't get along with every subsequent one—some were downright miserable to live with—at least no physical violence developed between us.

That little trip to the crisis unit cost me at least thirty dollars in canteen goods, no doubt stolen by Sick, but it was worth it. When the doctor finally decided I was no longer a threat to myself, I was returned to Building 9—but to a different cell.

The next day a CO brought me mail, including some letters postmarked more than two weeks earlier and visitor approval forms for Mom and Rick. I'd been waiting over a month to receive those. But it would be yet another month before I saw them. First I took another detour to the hole.

That happened because two inmates conspired to steal my canteen. With money my parents put in my prison account, I purchased two bags full of food, coffee, and personal care items. An inmate called me over to speak to him. While he distracted me, another inmate grabbed my sacks and took off running. When I turned and saw what was happening, I chased him. I tackled him, and we crashed to the ground, my possessions tumbling from the bags and scattering across the dirt.

We leaped to our feet and faced each other. I knew if I let him get away with this, I would continue to be victimized. And I just could not allow that. I swung at him, hitting his jaw. Immediately the alarm blared, and everyone dropped to the ground. A half dozen COs appeared and cuffed us.

A sergeant had witnessed the incident and described it to the captain. Because a great deal of this sort of thing had been going, the captain wanted me to press charges for strong-armed robbery.

I shook my head. "I'm not a snitch. If I press charges, that will follow me anywhere I go."

His eyebrows lifted. "What are you afraid of? You're already in SNY. This yard is full of snitches."

I spoke more firmly. "I've got a life sentence, and I'm not going to have the reputation of a snitch following me around the whole time."

He scowled. "Fine. You can go to the hole with him."

So off we went. Each to our own cell in hell.

This happened in October of 2007, when San Diego was—quite literally—burning. Because a state of emergency had been declared, the prison was locked down.

Through the window in my tiny cell, I watched the fire eat away the vegetation on nearby mountains. In the dark, orange flames crept down to the valley and licked up everything in their path. Smoke wafted through the air duct and slowly filled my cell. I coughed and covered my mouth and nose with my T-shirt. How messed up life was! Here I was, in prison with a life sentence for something I didn't do, in a smoke-filled cell in Ad-Seg for not snitching, while San Diego appeared to burn to the ground. *What next, God?*

Eventually the air cleared and I was able to read. I had access to only one book, and I was halfway through my third reading when I was finally let out. I suppose I'd been there four or five days.

A few days after I returned to Building 9, the guy I'd tackled approached me on the yard and apologized. He knew I could have pressed charges against him but didn't. The other inmates knew it, too. No one bothered me that way again.

I still hadn't seen my parents, and as the days turned into weeks my frustration grew. Inmates in Reception, like me, weren't allowed to call anyone or have contact visits, supposedly for security purposes. And because so many prisoners inhabited R. J. Donovan, visiting space and time were limited. The visiting room resembled those I'd used in county jail, rows of booths where you viewed visitors through thick glass and spoke to them through phone receivers—most of which didn't work. Here I saw Mom and Rick for the first time in nearly three months.

That visit raised my spirits and encouraged me. But it also filled me with sorrow. I loved seeing Mom and chatting with Rick, but I grieved not being able to hug them or leave with them.

After they learned how to navigate the arbitrary prison system rules, they visited me every Saturday and Sunday. Their goodbyes always pierced my spirit. I hated seeing their backs as they walked away.

Although I'd made spiritual progress in many ways prior to arriving at prison, my sentencing had turned me into an emotional, psychological, and religious disaster.

For Mom's birthday in 2007, I wrote a letter that expressed my spiritual distress:

Faith and love is the foundation we stand on in our relationship with God, but also with each other. I'm trying to learn by your example, but it's just so hard to see past these prison walls. Sometimes I feel as if my prayers are being held captive right along with me or I'm just praying to a silent and inactive God. I know in my heart that it isn't so, but Satan would have me believe otherwise. My wish is that God would just open my eyes to see his purpose for my life and the reason for what I am experiencing, because right now nothing makes any sense to me. I refuse to believe that it's to test my faith and make me stronger. Not I, you or anyone else involved. How could a loving God allow this to happen? Why can't his so-called unconditional love feel more like your unconditional love?

Attempting to view life through the eyes of my newly found faith frustrated me. I'd lived through all my craziness prior to incarceration without being seriously injured. How could I doubt God's mercy? My heart filled with shame for feeling bitterness toward my heavenly Father. I carried few physical scars from those reckless years, but many marred my heart and mind. If only God would heal those! Maybe then I'd feel like a new creation in Christ. According to the Bible, I was a new person. Yet I still gestated in faith's womb.

It was like having keys in your pocket to a brand new car and being told you're not allowed to drive it for an indefinite time, possibly never. I wanted to test drive my new life, but felt prohibited from doing so. I wanted to see the world again with the clarity I now had as a believer, with the enlightenment I received from the Bible and the Spirit. But I was confined inside a concrete box. My car had to stay parked in the garage.

In May of 2008, Rick contacted the California Innocence Project (CIP), which is an organization of attorneys and law students who investigate and litigate cases of wrongfully convicted prisoners. A week or so later, the CIP sent a lengthy pre-screen form that Rick helped me fill out and promptly return.

After months went by with no word from the CIP, Rick followed up with a phone call in November. He learned they had not yet reviewed my submission due to their heavy workload.

I now know that the California Innocence Project receives about 2,000 requests from inmates every year. Due to limited resources and staff, they can take on only a handful. But at the time, the delay fueled my frustration.

I grew angrier with God, at times verbally lashing out. "This is all wrong, Lord. I shouldn't be here. How could you let this happen to me? How can you let something like this happen to anyone?"

I felt God had let me down. I knew he owed me nothing. He had given me eternal life. Shouldn't that be enough?

But uncertainty invaded my mind. Had I really come to Christ in true faith or had I merely sought God because I wanted justice in the courtroom? I couldn't be sure and began to doubt my salvation. More than ever, I scrutinized the Bible, looking for an excuse to point the finger at God. That excuse came all right, but not from the Bible.

On December 12, 2008, I received a letter stating that my convictions had been affirmed by the State Court of Appeals. No legal recourse remained for me in the state of California. My only option would be to file a *habeas corpus* with the federal appeals court, which usually takes many years and has almost no chance of winning. Throughout my incarceration, the Lord had given me precious pearls of hope. But once again, the enemy snatched another pearl from me. By now, I felt the devil wore the finest and most priceless necklace in the universe.

Losing the appeal was all the ammunition I needed to load my mouth and shoot verbal bullets at God. And yet—surprising even myself—that's not what I did. Instead I wrote this to my parents:

> Today I received news of my convictions being affirmed by the court of appeal. Obviously, I am greatly disappointed by this. I want so badly to rage at God, the system which failed me, the man, the world and, yes, myself. But how can I? It's as if God isn't there, and if he is, why should he be bothered with such a petty matter as this? He's got the whole world to run. How shall an ungrateful sinner such as I confront and accuse the Almighty God for not intervening in my legal affairs? After all, he has done more than I could ever ask by sacrificing his beloved Son. But still it's not enough. I want more, more, more. So, I rage in my heart and mind against the Invisible God. How pointless and futile it is, I know, not to mention sinful, but to whom else do I go with these thoughts and feelings?

Earlier that day, I'd had a premonition and experienced distressing thoughts. It all seemed too much. I continued:

> I really feel as though I'm under attack here, and so I ask, where is God? I'm tired of reading about such a great God who never seems to be around when I really need him. And I'm tired of praying.

Perhaps I'm being punished for my lack of faith. So, now I have the pathetic justice system, the man, the world, and myself to rage at. But this too is pointless and futile. At least with God there's a possibility of being listened to and maybe even answered. I know I'm really my own worst enemy. I sabotage the peace of my salvation and impede the work of the Holy Spirit in my life, and because of it I have not the joy of the Lord and neither am I bearing any of the precious fruits of the Spirit. The Bible says that a branch cannot bear fruit of itself, unless it abides in the Vine, and the branch that does not bear fruit is taken away. So, where does that leave me, the withered and unproductive branch? They say there's only a foot between the heart and the mind, but it's the longest, most treacherous damned foot in the world.

Despite my doubt and discouragement, I still devoured the Bible daily, even doing a correspondence Bible study. I attended chapel services, read every piece of Christian or so-called Christian literature I could get my hands on, conversed with other brothers in Christ, and participated in evangelistic activities with non-Christian inmates. None of it seemed to make much difference. But without even knowing it, I was being refined in the crucible.

As the weeks and months dragged on, it seemed my time in Reception would never end. I wanted out badly, but I was also afraid to leave. I could only assume that violence toward sex offenders would be worse on a regular yard, where turnover was lower and everyone knew each other better.

My own cellie for six months, known as Oso (Spanish for bear), loved to torment sex offenders. He was very large—over six feet—and ate like a bear preparing to hibernate. He constantly spoke about this or that guy as a rapist or a cho-mo (child molester) and looked for ways to beat up or extort him. What made this so difficult to understand was that he had been involved in an inner city church ministry and planned to return to it after he'd served his time. He read the Bible, and we conversed about it almost daily.

Whenever he started going off about a sex offender, I'd appeal to him from the Bible, "God says vengeance is mine, I will repay," or I'd say, "We're all accountable to God and we have to let him deal with these guys." But I had to be careful not to make him suspect me.

Certain personnel often informed inmates who enjoyed tormenting sex offenders when one entered the building. On a couple of occasions, I even witnessed the COs facilitate an assault. One time the inmate's cell door was opened, and another inmate went in and beat him up—taking some of his canteen as he left—all in view of two floor officers and one in the guard tower. Another time a guy was shoved into the shower stall and pummeled while the same COs stood by and pretended not to see it.

The majority of officers did their job and stopped attacks if they saw one going down. That fact did not comfort me in the least. If my cover was ever pulled, it would take only seconds to receive life-threatening injury.

Because I was confined to my cell for long periods of time, I implemented a daily workout routine. It helped me feel more productive and sleep better as well as reducing stress, anxiety, and depression.

My routine consisted mostly of pushups and squats, but my favorite exercise utilized a water bag. I'd fill a new trash bag with water, then stuff it inside a T-shirt, tie a knot at the bottom, and use the sleeves as handles. Sometime I thrust a rolled-up magazine through the arm holes for a bar. This water bag worked great for doing curls. Trash bags were fairly easy to obtain from an inmate porter, but could be difficult to replace because they were considered contraband. When we left our cells for yard or to shower, COs often confiscated them, especially from inmates they particularly didn't like.

Common practice during facility-wide lockdowns was to strip-search inmates and ransack their cells. During one lockdown, my cellie and I watched the COs work their way closer to our cell, and I grew anxious about losing my beloved water bag. Certain it would be confiscated, I tried to add a little humor to the experience by writing on the water bag: "Please don't take me away, I promise I'll be good." I made the Os in "good" into eyes and drew a smiling face with a tongue hanging out.

Two male COs took my cellie and me out and searched us, while a female CO went into our cell. She soon signaled for us to return. She didn't have the water bag in hand, and it wasn't lying out on the tier.

As we approached, she began laughing. "In all my years as a prison guard, I've never seen that one." She grinned. "You can keep the bag."

I breathed a sigh of relief. "Thank you."

As I entered the cell, my water bag sat in the corner with the face smiling at me. The CO had not torn apart our cell as usually happened. This same CO was around all the time I was in prison and not once did I see her treat an inmate with contempt. She honored God in her calling by remaining professional and maintaining her integrity.

One day, I looked through the little glass window of my cell door and recognized an inmate being escorted through the sally port. It was Ralph, whom I had met and liked in county jail, although we hadn't been very close. The floor officers told Ralph where to find his cell, and he headed my way. He walked up the stairs and paused a few doors down from me.

I called out, "Hey, Ralph! It's Uriah."

He walked toward my door. "Uriah?"

"Yeah, Uriah Courtney. From county jail, the sixth floor."

"Sure. I remember you."

The CO urged him to move on, and I called after him. "I'll talk to you later."

Ralph arrived just in time. My current cellie and I hadn't been getting along, so I'd been looking for a new cellmate. We lived together for only a few months, but we became friends. And the Lord provided much opportunity for me to share the gospel with him. In the early morning hours on the day he was transferred to another prison, we prayed together. I asked the Lord to keep him safe and regenerate his heart to believe in Christ.

A couple of months later, I received a letter from him that my stepdad forwarded to me (inmates aren't allowed to write each other except for special circumstances). In that letter, he excitedly described how he had been born again and was not only reading the Bible, but also participating in a reputable correspondence Bible study course. The wonderful news thrilled me, and I thanked and praised God.

This confirmation of Christ's transforming power refreshed my faltering spirit and ignited the smoldering wick of my faith. I longed to be a light to those around me and clearly proclaim the gospel. I knew I hadn't been left alone in my present darkness to grope about as a blind man, but to be a beacon—however dim—so others too could find their way home to the true light. I wanted to reflect Christ as a lamp in which others might see a glimmer of Jesus, because it only takes the faintest ray of deity to pierce the blackest heart.

Because prisoners constantly flowed through Reception, I saw many inmates come and go. Some even got paroled and came back while I was still there. These poor souls wasting their lives grieved me, and I wanted to help them. I told them how much I wished I could be paroled, but would never be because I'd been wrongfully accused and given a life sentence. I urged them to get right with God and change their ways before they came back for life without another chance to parole. I prayed for them and with them, asking the Lord to come into their hearts and regenerate them.

One of these men, Chris, seemed to have a genuine desire to change his lifestyle and attend church when he got out. We prayed together early on the morning of his release, and I sincerely hoped he would stay out this time and find a good church.

Unfortunately, I saw him again just a couple months later, back in on another parole violation. The only church he'd attended had been a chapel service in county jail, led by the Budloves. He told me they sent their greetings. He also said they had shared my testimony in chapel that day, including the charges I had been accused and convicted of.

The Budloves intended only to proclaim Christ's transformative power in my life and how he sustained me as I continued to fight for justice. They didn't realize, however, that sharing such information with other inmates could have brought about disastrous consequences for me. Chris said not to worry; he wouldn't mention it. He believed the Budloves' story and that I was telling the truth about being falsely accused.

After another month or two, Chris was either paroled or sent to another prison. Apparently he kept his word, because not one inmate gave me any trouble. Once again, God kept me safe.

My mind often envisioned God's protection like the surrounding hills mentioned in Psalm 121 and the mountains I viewed through my cell's window. Peering out at God's creation made me feel closer to him, but also flooded me with melancholy memories of past outdoor experiences. I'd recall how alive I'd felt then—how much nature stimulated my senses. What a luxury to be outdoors! Now I was reduced to looking at a not-so-beautiful sliver of world through a dirty prison window.

One evening, I read in Hebrews, ending with chapter 11. I stared at the darkness outside my window and pondered the first verse, "Now faith is the substance of things hoped for, the evidence of things not seen" (NKJV). Having difficulty living out the Christian faith, I was profoundly affected by this verse. I mused about it for over an hour and wrote down my thoughts:

> Faith is an enigma. Actually it's the faith necessary to please God and be acceptable in his sight that is an enigma. From where does this type of faith come? Is it placed in the believer's heart because God sees his desire for him, or is it something the believer produces on his own? Being a man who responds to senses, I feel it impossible to produce the faith necessary to believe in a God who is not tangible. If I can't see, touch, taste, hear, or smell something, how can I believe it exists? When I look out my window at night, I see lights pulsing in the distance. I can't see the actual source,

but I can see the light and therefore deduce the light must have a source. I have faith that the source exists because I can see the light. I watch it pulse and shimmer; I see a traffic light change from green to yellow to red. But I can't see God or apprehend him with any of my senses; yet I still believe he exists and is the creator of the universe. Why? I do not know. My guess, however ignorant, is that he has given me the faith one must have to believe in his existence. That would be the substance mentioned in Hebrews 11:1, and if there is substance to something then there is evidence. Substance and evidence are building blocks of faith, placed in the believer's heart and mind to diligently seek God, by God.

While in Reception, I chafed at the delay in being assigned to a yard. Most inmates spend only three or four months in Reception, but I'd remain a total of twenty-one months, which is extremely rare. I didn't understand why God kept me there so long, but this was the Lord's blessed providence to work things out according to his purpose.

Prior to leaving county jail in June of 2007, I'd read a newspaper article about the state opening up a Level 4 SNY yard at Donovan. At the time, I'd thought little of it because I had no intention of going SNY. But now I was SNY at Donovan, waiting for the State to determine the facility to which I'd be endorsed. And the whole time I was in Reception, the prison was renovating the adjoining yard for Level 4 SNY inmates.

I pleaded with the Lord to keep me at Donovan. Mom and Rick lived only about fifteen minutes away, and Mom often mentioned how she could see the prison's lights when she drove home from work at night along the Silver Strand. Visiting me in another facility would burden them, but inmates are frequently sent hundreds of miles away from family.

After months of waiting and prayers from many people who knew about the situation, the Lord answered. One day, the counselor told me that I had been endorsed to R. J. Donovan, C Yard. Still, I lacked confidence in actually seeing that happen.

On February 10, 2009, I read in my cell as usual. We'd been on a facility-wide lockdown for some time, and there wasn't much else to do.

A CO came to my door. "Courtney, roll up all your property and get ready to move."

My heart pounded as I jumped down from my bunk. "Where am I going?"

"You're going to C Yard."

I punched the air and exclaimed, "Yes!"

As I packed up all my worldly possessions, I whispered prayers to God, praising him for keeping me at Donovan. Although much violence existed there, it wasn't a hardcore prison like some others in California. I asked the Lord to please keep me safe and to bless me with a compatible cellmate.

The door opened, and I said goodbye to my cellie. While I walked down the stairs with my property in tow, some inmates wished me well.

Before we left the building, the CO set down a garbage bag full of CDCR (California Department of Corrections and Rehabilitation) blues. He told me and a few other guys, who were also moving, to find things that fit and put them on.

At last, I was shedding the bright orange Reception outfit and donning prison blues. Only I couldn't find pants that fit. I had to grab some string to fasten a pair around my waist. Then I picked up my belongings and walked through the sally port of Building 9 for the last time.

It was exactly four years and two days after my arrest in Texas.

16

New Beginnings

Richard J. Donovan Correctional Facility, C Yard

My mind raced during the five-minute walk from Building 9 to Building 14. I was about to enter a Level 4 yard, and Sensitive Needs Yard or not, Level 4s are notorious for extreme violence and brutality. As I entered the sally port, I prayed repeatedly for the Lord to provide me with a decent cellie.

A CO directed me up the stairs. The door opened as I approached the cell, and out stepped a tall, muscular guy who appeared to be in his fifties. Tattoos covered his visible skin.

Oh, Lord, not again. Not another Sick. Or something even worse.

He jerked his head toward me. "Hey, you need to let the COs know you need a mattress."

"Okay." I turned and called to the CO. "I'm going to need a mattress."

My new cellie stuck out his hand. "My name's Johnny."

"Uriah." I shook his hand and decided to immediately dispel any notion that I might be a rapist or a cho-mo. "I'm a lifer. I was convicted of kidnapping and robbery."

He told me what he was in for and added, "I'm a lifer, too."

After we chatted for a bit, he said, "I'm planning on moving a buddy in with me the next time the program office does convenience moves."

My heart sank. All too soon I'd have to go through this moving process again.

The door opened and the CO brought in the thin pad that passed for a mattress. My cellie waved toward the empty upper bunk. "Go ahead and get settled in."

The first thing I did was arrange my books and personal items on a shelf.

Johnny looked over my shoulder. "What kind of books you got there?"

I showed him my Bible and study books, explaining that I was a Christian. Then I made up the bed, all the while taking in my new environment. Like many inmates, my new cellmate appeared a bit compulsive. The floor was spotless, the sink wiped dry and gleaming, and all his belongings neatly in place. A TV sat on his shelf and a radio on the desk.

He walked over to the desk. "You want to listen to the radio?"

"Sure. I haven't heard any music since I left county jail almost two years ago."

He turned on a classic rock station. Led Zepplin's "Stairway to Heaven" filled the cell. The sweet sound of singing guitars created within me an odd mix of euphoria and melancholy. Vivid memories of my younger days flashed through my mind. I almost felt high. My senses had been deprived of music for so long that I had difficulty processing it. It soon became too much to bear, but I didn't want to say anything.

After a while, Johnny asked, "Would you like to watch TV?"

I sighed with relief. "Fine."

While he watched a show, I sat down and wrote my parents a quick letter, telling them the good news that I was still at Donovan.

Johnny continued watching TV until late into the night. I lay in bed, thanking God that I had finally made it to a program yard and would be staying near my parents. Normally inmates wear headphones to avoid disturbing their cellies, but Johnny's were broken. I wondered if I'd be able to fall asleep with this strange but familiar sound. Eventually I did and slept well.

The next morning we came off lockdown, and I walked to the chow hall for the first time. With nearly a thousand inmates per yard, the experience overwhelmed me. Hundreds of men filed into the two dining areas or waited for their turn to eat.

Johnny and I stood in a long line of inmates stretching out the building and halfway across the yard. Nearly everyone greeted him with deference. I was relieved he seemed well-respected but anxious that he knew so many inmates. The more people he knew, the more would be curious about his new cellie. And anonymous was what I wanted to be.

The noise in the chow hall deafened me. We grabbed our breakfast trays and brown paper sack lunches and sat at an octagon metal table with four seats.

Johnny motioned to the guy sitting across from me. "This is Brian. He's a Christian, too."

I nodded at the man. "Uriah."

Johnny said, "Brian's looking for a different cellie."

I looked at Brian with new interest. "That right?"

He returned my gaze. "You're a Christian, huh?"

"Yeah."

"We might cell up together."

"Might." I was cautious.

"Maybe we should get to know each other better first."

"That'd be a good idea. We can talk about it more later."

As I walked back to Building 14, I looked around the yard. Fear and loneliness stabbed my heart. *This is it. This is the end of the road until my life is over, or until God changes something.*

*

Even now, recalling those feelings makes me shudder. A deep depression darkened my spirit to the point that I didn't care whether I lived or died. Dying seemed preferable. Then I would be with my Lord in heaven where there would be no more tears, pain, fear, anxiety, or injustice.

Yet I praised the Lord for allowing me to remain at Donovan. Even in my deeply depressed state, I realized this affirmed God's care for me.

Johnny described C Yard as pretty laid back, although gang drama and violence still occurred, and he cautioned me about choosing friends wisely. As a new arrival, I was on Orientation status and wouldn't be permitted to go on the yard, to the dayroom, or have visits. I was so thankful to finally have a real program that I didn't care, except for visits.

Only a week after my arrival, I moved in with Brian, the guy I'd met at that first breakfast. I immediately noticed that he owned many thick volumes of Bible commentaries and theological works.

After I settled in, I sat on my rack, sipping a prized cup of Folgers instant coffee and watching Brian. He was a short and skinny guy with an awkward-looking goatee. He fluttered around the cell like a bird that couldn't find a place to rest, adjusting his homemade TV antenna. A square of aluminum cut from a soda can had been flattened and jammed against the tiny cell window. Paper clips and wire stretched out from it, eventually snaking together into a coaxial cable to his TV. The contraption looked like a dysfunctional spider's web.

When our cell door opened for breakfast the next morning, we stepped out and waited for the order to start walking. The inmate from the cell next to ours hurried over to introduce himself as Jonathan Childers.

With still-tousled tufts of gray hair on the sides of his head, he appeared to have just woken up. But his eyes gleamed as he handed me a gospel tract and asked, "Do you know the Lord?"

I took the tract and shook his hand. "Why, yes, I do know the Lord. I'm a believer in Christ."

It soon became apparent that Jonathan's purpose was evangelism. I often saw him passing out tracts or talking to other inmates. I learned he was a lifer, for murdering his own parents. I couldn't comprehend how that gentle man had committed such a horrible crime. But since he lived "next door," I got to know him pretty well and discovered that small man had a gigantic heart for Christ and sharing the gospel.

Brian and I began adjusting to each other. Like me, he was an ex-tweaker. Unfortunately, he remained mentally stuck in that mode. He loved to talk all the time, which initially annoyed me. Sometimes I wanted silence in order to concentrate. Eventually he got the clue: don't bother Uriah while he's studying.

But I often felt inclined to conversation, and we had some enlightening ones. Brian had a sharp intellect and a firm grip on biblical theology. Within our first few days living together, we were discussing specific texts at length.

He said, "You're the first cellie I've had in a long time who holds biblical views similar to my own." He waved toward the books on his shelf. "You can read any of my books any time you like."

The first one I picked up was *Behold, He Cometh*, a commentary on the book of Revelation by Herman Hoeksema. I had longed to understand the metaphors and symbolic language of John's visions, and that book helped me comprehend Revelation better than ever before. It also quickened my resolve to dig deeper into studying the end times, which I learned was the branch of theology called eschatology.

Then I moved on to a three-volume set, *The Triple Knowledge*, by the same author. It affected my thinking profoundly, more than any book other than the Bible up to that time. It's a commentary on the masterfully crafted Heidelberg Catechism, whose three parts (Guilt, Grace, and Gratitude) mirror the construction of the book of Romans. This beautiful catechism changed my life, piquing my spiritual hunger. It was like my second great awakening.

During the six months Brian and I were cellies, I practically swallowed each of his books. The Spirit enlightened my mind and swept away much of my confusion about certain passages of Scripture.

Was my spiritual depression over? Not by any means. I felt like the Ephesian church Christ described in Revelation 2:4, "But I have this against you, that you have abandoned the love you had at first."

My passion for Christ had become cold and mechanical. I obediently read my Bible daily and prayed regularly. But I had no love in my heart. I believed in God, but I'm not sure I trusted the God I professed to believe in. His infallible Word should have been my soul's anchor, keeping me from being tossed to and fro by the calamities around and within me. But I tumbled on rocks of offence and tripped on stones of stumbling (1 Pet 2:8). Why? Because I took my eyes off Christ and his finished work on the cross.

Brian's books opened my mind to realize these truths. God used them to help me physically, psychologically, and spiritually survive my remaining years in prison. Could God have sustained me another way? Certainly. But I'm glad he didn't, because my life was—and still is—richly blessed by those theologians, especially the ancient church fathers I came to love and admire.

On March 3, 2009, I finally went to Committee, was taken off Orientation, and given a custody status. Because I was a lifer with a rape conviction and an escape charge, my points were high. I received the status with the most restrictions.

I was not permitted yard time on weekends or dayroom at night and on weekends. My phone usage was limited to one call per month (although some generous COs allowed me to use it more often so sometimes I could call both Dad and Colton in the same month). Only a couple of educational classes and job options were available for me. I had to be in my cell every day at noon for a special head count. If I or any other inmate with the same status missed this count, the program would be shut down and all inmates would have to return to their cells.

The time I spent outside my cell during a full week added up to about eight hours, often less. Despite the limitations imposed by my status, I was thrilled. At last, I'd get visitation privileges. And not behind smudged and blurry glass through broken telephones. No, I was going to get *contact* visits!

After Committee, I dashed off a letter to my parents, telling them the wonderful news and that we could possibly see each other the following weekend. Now I was also allowed to receive quarterly packages, so I asked them to order some food and other things from approved vendors.

I know some people think inmates should have nothing. Why give these criminals any creature comforts? Let me just say that if these few items were not given to prisoners, there would be far more violence than already exists. Instead of a handful of pathetic animals, there would be hordes of evil beasts. Even with these small privileges, a man has to struggle to keep his sanity and some sense of dignity.

The day of visitation came at last. The door to my cell slid open, and the tower officer's voice echoed through the loudspeaker in the dayroom, "Courtney, you have a visit." I was so nervous that my hands trembled.

A CO escorted me to the visiting center for C Yard. Upon entering, I was handed off to another CO, who gave me a quick pat down and then walked me to a steel door. He unlocked it with a large skeleton-style key and swung it open. Mom and Rick stared at me.

Mom cried out, "Oh, my goodness! There he is!" She rushed at me with arms wide open. I hadn't had physical contact with my mom or any family member in over four years. I needed to feel her embrace like I needed oxygen to breathe. Rick threw his arms around us. Because hugs must be brief (and are limited to the beginning and end of visits), it lasted only a matter of seconds. But it was a priceless moment.

We talked about family and friends, my legal issues, the new yard and its privileges, the Bible, and more. We were thrilled and grateful to sit in each other's physical presence, not separated by glass or any other obstruction.

My parents purchased refreshments from a vendor at the prison. For the first time since I'd been incarcerated, I enjoyed real food: pizza, hot wings, chocolate cake, and a soda. I was stuffed to the point of nausea.

When our allotted time was over, we all hugged and said our goodbyes. My parents promised to return the next day, which was Sunday.

As I stood by the door, waving at Mom and Rick while they exited in the opposite direction, such powerful joy filled my heart that it almost hurt. That pain increased when I considered the bleak existence on the door's other side. I walked through the door, and it closed. A curtain of sorrow descended.

The CO said, "Take off all your clothes."

I knew the routine. I unlaced my shoes, took them off, and handed them to the CO. Then I slipped off my socks, shirt, pants, and underwear. I stood naked before the CO, while he searched my clothes for drugs or contraband.

When he finished, he dropped them to the dirty floor. "Lift your genitals, bend over, spread your cheeks, and cough."

The horrible embarrassment at having to go through this indignity had long passed. You just go through the motions. Most of the COs merely went through the motions, too. It was their job to prevent drugs from getting into the prison, and this was part of it.

But one CO in particular delighted in these strip searches. He was by far the most disrespectful CO I had the displeasure of being around. And we saw a lot of each other because he not only worked at the visiting center, but also in my building.

When I returned from a visit one day at the same time as two other inmates known for illegal activities, this CO was working in the guard tower of our building. He didn't want to let us in. I said something about that, and he didn't like it. In front of the other two, he called me a "f . . . ing cho-mo."

When I stared at him in surprise, he said, "Yeah, you know what I'm talking about."

Of course, I denied it. The other two just looked at me and shook their heads. The door opened, and they said some choice words about the CO, evidently not believing what he'd said. Neither of them ever mentioned it again, and I was never bothered by anyone else about my charges. God's protective hedge still surrounded me.

And God's sanctifying work continued in me. On numerous occasions during my incarceration, I struggled with a bad cellie or felt threatened by another inmate or a sadistic CO. These situations generated great mental or spiritual turmoil, but I found that after a process of much prayer and patience either that person or I would be removed. God always did this.

For my entire first year of contact visits, anxiety plagued me. Here I sat, finally face-to-face with Mom and Rick, but my mind was taken over by things I can't describe. Sometimes I could barely keep from fleeing. Those anxiety attacks were the most debilitating feelings I've ever had. Although I eagerly anticipated weekly visits, they left me emotionally drained.

One weekend, Mom brought along my nephew Tre, who was eleven. At the time, it wasn't clear if I could have visits from minors. Since they had let Tre in, we'd figured it was okay and talked for about a half hour.

The ombudsman, Marti, making her rounds, came over and we introduced Tre, mentioning our uncertainty about his visit. She said she'd look into it and left the room.

Only moments later, a CO came to our table. Looking at Mom, he said, "Your visit has been terminated. You need to leave immediately."

My face flushed with embarrassment, and my heart lurched with fear. Other visitors would wonder why the visit ended so suddenly and they'd ask questions. Inmates might assume I'd done something inappropriate.

I stopped by the program office to see if the sergeant or someone else could find out what was going on. Having learned very little there, I returned to my building, agonizing over the possibilities: *Will my visiting privileges be revoked? Am I going to get written up or sent to the hole? Will the other inmates finally find out that I was convicted of rape?*

Soon after I returned to my cell, the door opened and I went to the dayroom, where Marti sat. I hurried over. "What happened? Am I in trouble?"

She shook her head. "Don't worry, Uriah. Your visits aren't going to be canceled."

I sat down, relief washing over me. "Thank God."

We talked about my prison experience in general for a few minutes. Then she inquired about my charges.

Without going into detail, I gave her a cut-and-paste picture. I didn't like discussing legalities with anyone who might be a potential witness for the prosecution should my case ever go back to court. I also knew she was responsible for my visit being terminated. I realized she had only done her job, but the sting was too fresh. I was very guarded in my conversation, even though we talked for about an hour.

When we discussed the possibility of parole, Marti commented that the board would want to hear the inmate express remorse. "If you don't admit responsibility, you will never get out."

I looked her in the eye. "Then I guess I'll spend the rest of my life in prison, because I will never admit to something I didn't do."

Years later, Marti communicated with my parents following my exoneration. She told them that after hearing me say those words, she went to her office and cried.

A couple of days after meeting with Marti, I was able to see my counselor and learned that I was not permitted visits with minors due to my charges. Pain and anger crushed me. I couldn't bear the thought of not seeing or holding my son or any of my nieces or nephews until they were eighteen. I raged against the system for taking away this last bit of hope about seeing Colton.

But I tried to submit my will to God in this, as in all things, asking him to heal my pain and help me grow in my faith.

Brian told me about a new Bible study group led by a deacon from Christ United Reformed Church in Santee and two students from Westminster Seminary in Escondido. I didn't immediately feel compelled to attend, but after hearing for a couple of weeks how much Brian enjoyed it, I could no longer deny the Spirit's prompting. I sent in a request to the counselor.

An inmate must first receive permission before participating in anything. Then he will be placed on a ducat list, and the pass will be given to him either the day of or the day before. After submitting my request, I was told only that I was on the waiting list.

A few days later, I left the medical clinic at the time the Bible study was meeting. I decided to peek into the chapel, which was part of the same building. The main room of the chapel was nearly empty, except for a few Muslims talking to each other.

Passing the Muslim inmates with their prayer blankets spread on the floor, I walked to the back of the chapel and entered a small room. Three leaders and about a dozen inmates sat in chairs lining the walls. Brian signaled for me to sit near him. I slipped in and listened to the discussion.

The class was still in its infancy, and both leaders and inmates asked many questions. The leaders were attempting to get a feel for this strange environment and what the prisoners sought, while we bombarded them with theological questions.

Some men wondered if meeting in the main chapel might be an option because the room's small size dictated the waiting list for would-be participants, like me. Scheduling conflicts existed, however, because the chapel was shared by all religions, even Satanists. The only exception was Native Americans, whose ceremonies took place in a small, fenced-off area of the yard. (I found it appealing to think of worshipping God outdoors under blue sky and the sun's natural light.)

The very next week I received a pass to attend the new group. Before each study began, one of our teachers led us in prayer. I loved hearing them pray. They spoke the language of the Bible with reverential awe.

After only a couple more classes, the seminary students could no longer come, due—I think—to a conflict with their class schedules and the time allotted to us in the tiny room. Now only the deacon led. I hope this doesn't sound sacrilegious, but learning from Alex as he taught us often felt to me like the apostles learning from Jesus in the upper room.

Alex endeavored to help us know Christ personally and experientially. He'd frequently tell us about the previous Sunday's sermon by Pastor Mike Brown at Christ URC. Alex seemed to hold Pastor Brown in high regard and recounted his sermons in great detail.

Alex also told us that Michael Horton, a professor at Westminster Seminary, often taught at that church. Dr. Horton had written many theological works, and Alex frequently articulated points from his books that related to our discussions. I imagined what it would be like to sit under Pastor Brown's preaching or listen to Dr. Horton's teaching. *Someday*, I thought, *I hope that actually comes to fruition.*

Those thoughts grew more and more as the Bible study went on. Alex brought in printed portions of Dr. Horton's not-yet-released book *The Christian Faith*. He brought in old and new copies of *Modern Reformation* magazine and CDs of the "White Horse Inn" radio show.

As word spread about this Bible study, the waiting list grew. Many hearts hungered for solid spiritual food and drink. We longed to eat meat. Milk was for babes, and we had grown lactose intolerant.

With administration no longer able to deny such a long list of names, the head chaplain finally secured a time slot for us in the main chapel. That was an exciting and happy day for Alex and the apostles.

I usually arrived at the chapel first. As soon as my door opened, I'd practically run across the yard in order to have a few moments of Alex's full attention. Perhaps I was being a little selfish, but I had many questions that I wanted to ask out of the hearing of other inmates. He offered comforting biblical wisdom and encouraged me to trust the Lord.

As men arrived, I'd watch them enter with joy flooding my heart. Blacks, whites, Hispanics. Such a beautiful sight. Our first meeting in the main chapel included about thirty men, and the following week around forty attended. Now that the number had grown to such a sizeable group, Alex said he wanted to teach us the Heidelberg Catechism.

Although this was a Bible study, the catechism served as a tool to teach us how to apply God's standards to our lives. Even today, I'm certain that if more churches used such creeds and confessions for instructing their flock, the church would be in a much better state.

Meanwhile, I found it increasingly difficult to live with Brian. He believed his conviction was unjust, which I could certainly relate to. But his bitterness and anger harmed his Christian witness. He knew doctrine, but failed to apply biblical principles to daily living.

After about six months, I began searching for another cellie. The thought of moving again frightened me. I don't like change, and you never know if you'll end up in a worse situation. I liked a few guys, but their cellies said they were difficult to live with.

Early one Saturday morning, while on my way for a visit with Mom and Rick, I saw Jonathan standing in one of those little cages. Seeing this gentle man in that cage caused both grief and anger.

I walked toward him. His head was bowed and his lips moved.

He's probably praying. I came up to the cage. "Jonathan, buddy, what's going on?"

He looked up and smiled. "Oh, I'm not in any trouble. I'm only here because my cellie drank too much and flipped out. Now the COs are investigating the matter."

I shook my head. "Sorry to hear that, man. I hope they let you out soon."

He shrugged. "I can still pray." And he went back to it.

After a couple days passed, I heard his cellie wouldn't be returning. I came to Jonathan's cell and spoke through the door.

"Jonathan, would you let me move in with you?"

"Sure," he said. "But you'll have to handle it."

"Don't worry." I nodded. "I'll take care of it."

A little later, I asked the CO if I could move in with Jonathan Childers.

"Is it okay with Childers?"

"Yes."

"I'll see what I can do."

But a week went by and nothing happened. That next Saturday, I told Mom and Rick how disappointed I was with myself for not being more proactive about the move. Later that same day, bed moves were done. A guy was escorted out of Ad-Seg and into Jonathan's cell. I chided myself for not taking advantage of the opportunity the Lord had provided.

The very next day, while I sat writing at my desk, a CO came to the door. "Courtney, pack up your belongings and move next door to 126."

I couldn't believe this was happening. At the very moment I'd been dwelling on my missed opportunity, I was told to move next door.

God used Brian to introduce me to biblical Christianity and a small library of books that ignited my flickering faith and reformed my thinking. Through him I met other brothers in Christ, like Robert, who would become a close friend, and Vance, who had expedited my entry into the Bible study. Then God placed me with Jonathan, who showed me how to apply biblical principles to my difficulties.

Less than ten days after I moved in with Jonathan, a CO came by our cell about 8:00 at night. "Roll up your property right now. You're being moved to Building 15."

Both of us were shocked. We'd done nothing wrong and had just settled in comfortably with each other. Why were we being moved?

Jonathan immediately started praying. After a couple of minutes, I tugged on his sleeve. "Let's go, brother. You've got to get your things rolled up and ready to move." Poor Jonathan, who has Asperger's Syndrome, was in such a sad state that he could barely get himself organized.

I helped him pack up his property. He had dozens of manila envelopes stuffed full of gospel tracts, prayer sheets, old mail, and biblical materials. Seeing all the envelopes and legal writing tablets filled with names of folks he'd prayed for throughout the years astonished me.

I took down our laundry line, made from the string in the elastic waistband of boxer shorts. I had collected extra blankets to wrap around the thin mattress for additional padding, but the mattress had to stay in the cell, so I quickly unlaced the blankets I had carefully tied around it.

All our books, personal care items, and other possessions were loaded into a large plastic buggy that was often used for hauling trash. I pushed the buggy from Building 13 to Building 15, which was the one farthest from the main gate and everything else.

The sun had long set and the night sky proclaimed God's glory. His handiwork in the heavens comforted me somewhat.

After we entered the sally port, we were told to go to cell 115. This disappointed me because I preferred the second tier. It was more quiet and private, and the window usually offered a better view.

For two hours that night and several the next day, I cleaned the walls, sink, toilet, and floor. I strung new laundry and towel lines and rigged a privacy curtain for using the toilet and taking birdbaths.

Many inmates who couldn't shower as frequently as they liked used a birdbath routine similar to mine. I rolled up a towel and laid it in front of the door to prevent water escaping onto the tier. The outside covering of an old coaxial cable served as a hose. I inserted the end of the hose into the small hole of the sink and jammed the water button on with a piece of plastic for continual flow. Sitting on or straddling the toilet, I'd wash myself and rinse off. Most of the water ran down the bowl, but a lot of it flowed onto the floor. So after I finished, I'd soak up the water with the floor towel and wring it out.

I actually took more birdbaths than real showers because dayroom and yard access often occurred at the same time, and I wasn't allowed out of my cell enough the way it was. I wanted to be outdoors, which meant I had to forego dayroom and shower time.

Moving can be very difficult. You must settle into a different cell and get it all set up the way you like it. You walk into a whole new situation with a different set of COs, who don't know you and often automatically treat you like a troublemaker. The inmates are new, the rules are slightly different, and the whole dynamic may change. You have to notify anyone with whom you correspond of your change in address. Mail will still get to you, but it will be even slower than normal.

Our move caused stress and anxiety for me, but it nearly traumatized Jonathan. After he settled down, however, he found a whole host of new inmates to evangelize.

I had been a Christian now for about five years, and my friendship with Jonathan became the greatest experience of brotherly love yet. Truly, he was a man after God's own heart, and it was a privilege living with him.

He continually added new names to his prayer sheets. When we watched the news or a TV show, Jonathan wrote down names of people to pray for. Out on the yard, he collected names of inmates and their friends and families. He prayed for the COs, nurses, and doctors. Some days he prayed for hours, stopping only to grab a bite to eat or something to drink. And his preferred method of praying was out loud.

I didn't mind so much, and we agreed that he could pray aloud as long as I wasn't studying. Sometimes, if I had on headphones while watching TV or listening to the radio, I would take them off so I could listen to him pray.

How moving to hear him pour out his heart, pleading with God to convert a sinner to Christ!

Building 15 may have been the farthest away from everything on the yard, but it was the first to go to chow hall. For breakfast, this was a good thing. I'd wake early, make a cup of instant coffee, and read the Bible until we left for breakfast. Our dinner time was often around 4:00, however, which was a little too early in my book.

But Jonathan and I began praying together after dinner, and that helped me overcome my remaining struggles with prayer. He always prayed for my family and that I would receive justice. At first, I had to gently remind him that unless he cut the prayers shorter, I might fall asleep.

For the first few months we lived together, I thought how blessed I was, but God revealed that his blessing extended beyond me.

One of an inmate's greatest tragedies is to be forgotten. This often causes a downward spiral into drunkenness, drug addiction, and sexual immorality, which widens the chasm between the inmate and his loved ones until no bridge could possibly span it.

As on only child, Jonathan—of course—had no family left and hadn't had a visitor in many years. After I shared his story with my parents, Rick offered to visit him once or twice a month while Mom visited me.

After Rick's first visit, Jonathan's visage transformed. His eyes brightened and he became more alert. Now he had something to look forward to—a brother in Christ to speak and eat with him.

Jonathan was the only inmate and cellie I trusted implicitly. But I didn't share details of my case or mention a rape charge even to him, because he was so honest and naïve he might have revealed the whole truth if another inmate tried to trick him by asking about my charges. His is the epitome of childlike faith.

Prior to his incarceration, Jonathan attended seminary and earned his Master of Divinity degree. He had studied under the Lutheran professor Dr. Rod Rosenbladt, whom we heard almost daily on the White Horse Inn radio program. In addition to listening to that show and R. C. Sproul's Renewing Your Mind, we studied together every day. We would read through the entire Bible, including the study notes. Then we'd discuss a book on systematic theology or a biblical subject before returning to the Bible. This was our routine for over three years.

Asperger's caused Jonathan some problems, but his phenomenal memory enabled him to give opposing views and interpretations from a host of theologians. As I listened to him expound Scripture, I was always amazed at the amount of detail he articulated. The way he tied together political, geographical, biblical, and personal facts increased my understanding and enlivened our conversations about church history.

Sadly, our Bible study with Alex ended only about a year after it began, due to some lame "security issue" excuse. Jonathan and I depended more than ever on the White Horse Inn broadcasts, but about a year later those stopped as well. I wrote to Dr. Horton, expressing my grief over the loss of this biblical teaching. He sent me a copy of his newly released *The Christian Faith*. I was honored to receive such a wonderful gift.

One morning I particularly regretted our cell's location on the first tier. I sat at my desk, drinking a large cup of coffee and reading the Bible. The men in the cell block began to stir and toilets started flushing. A clog in the system caused it to back up and overflow into our cell.

I hurriedly gathered up our belongings from the floor and put them on our beds to keep them out of the raw sewage now flowing like a river over the floor and under the cell door into the dayroom. I hollered in the air vent for the guys to stop flushing, but it was too late. Our toilet overflowed for many long minutes.

At last, a CO opened my door and allowed me to get a mop, a bucket, and some rubber gloves to clean up the mess. I could barely keep from vomiting. I sanitized the entire cell the best I could with a strong chemical cleaner. After finishing the disgusting task, I asked the CO if I could take a hot shower. I felt completely contaminated and thought surely he would grant my request. He didn't.

His denial baffled me. I wondered why any human with even a shred of decency would not allow someone the dignity of cleansing their body after dealing with raw sewage.

Although I experienced a few instances of such baffling behavior, I also appreciated COs who granted small favors that made a huge difference in our lives. A few facilitated my new love affair with books.

Because hardcover books are not permitted in prison, the inmate receiving one is often given the choice of either returning the book or allowing the CO to cut off the cover. But sometimes a CO didn't care or notice, and we occasionally received a hardcover book.

I confess I owned a few of these. Surprisingly, I built up quite a theological library in prison.

One day an inmate approached me and offered to let me buy Matthew Henry's six-volume commentary on the entire Bible—all six volumes retaining their hard covers. The thought of having nearly 5,000 pages of fine print, theological meat made me salivate. Forgive me for this comparison, but the rush I felt at the prospect of owning this commentary equaled shooting up a large dose of crystal meth. I had to have those books.

After negotiating the price, I held the volumes in my hands. What a treasure! The best-selling commentary by a great Puritan theologian. I carefully arranged them on the shelf containing my growing library.

The day before my birthday in 2010, I returned from a visit to find some new books on my bunk. A few I had ordered, but those didn't grab my attention. What did was an ESV John MacArthur Study Bible, sitting there in all its glory. The CO had even left the nice protective box it came in. I can't describe how the sight of that Bible thrilled me. I opened the box and touched my name, embossed in gold print, on the genuine leather cover. Mom and Rick had sent it as a birthday gift. I still use that same study Bible.

The entire time I adjusted to C Yard and experienced a new beginning in my Christian faith, God was working behind the scenes to deliver me from more than my spiritual depression.

17

Budding Hope

Richard J. Donovan Correctional Facility, C Yard

On Easter Sunday of 2010, Jonathan and I spoke about the significance of the day and celebrated it with our own worship. That afternoon we lay on our bunks, watching a movie on TV. Then the earthquake hit.

At first I thought Jonathan was pressing up against the bottom of my bunk with his hands or feet. When the entire building began rocking, I realized we were having a good quake.

How exciting! I jumped off my bunk and raced to the window. Could I see the surface of the surrounding hills ripple? The tall light poles surrounding the prison swaying? But the quake hit hard and fast and was over in seconds, so I saw no visible signs outside. I turned back to survey our cell.

Jonathan stared at me with a pale face. His hands shook as he fumbled to sit up. "Oh, my, Uriah! I think this might be the Big One."

I chuckled. "Don't think so, Jonathan. Not yet anyway."

I wished it were the Lord returning. The concrete walls and roof might collapse on our heads, but that would end my miserable existence and I'd be with him.

Although aftershocks rocked the building, this didn't appear to be the day of Christ's return. Noticing the TV inching closer to the edge of its shelf, I dashed over to keep it from falling. If today wasn't going to be the great day of the Lord, I wasn't about to lose that TV.

*

While I longed for any release from my prison existence, my hope for exoneration had begun to bud. By the time the earthquake hit, it was almost two years after Rick's initial contact with the California Innocence Project. And during the previous year, God had been working.

Early in 2009, Rick had written another letter, suggesting that my case was a "highly probable candidate" for "touch DNA analysis." He also wrote that my conviction had been based only on conflicting eyewitness testimony.

In March of 2009, I received a letter from the California Innocence Project requesting any information that would be helpful in their assessment. This was while I was still on Orientation status and wasn't allowed visits. But in God's providence, I was called out for a no-contact visit with Rick, which enabled me to relay the request to him in a timely manner.

In Rick's response to the CIP, he explained how we now realized that my attorneys had looked at only my personal cell phone record, but I had been using a company phone during that period. Rick had documented my phone use and corroborated all calls with sworn declarations from the people I spoke to on November 24, including the exact time frame of the attack. He had reviewed the trial transcript, and he believed my legal counsel had been "negligent and provided a poor defense." He'd also reviewed the detective's investigation notes, which demonstrated his inaccuracies during the trial. Rick reiterated the need for new DNA testing on the victim's clothing, and concluded, "I have no doubt that my son is innocent of this charge and is the victim of a classic case of False Eyewitness ID."

My hope blossomed on January 26, 2010, when the California Innocence Project opened my case. This didn't mean they would take it on, but they did begin to gather evidence. Because the CIP is associated with the California Western School of Law in San Diego, a law student is assigned to each case. Amber, the first student on my case, contacted my trial and appeal attorneys and obtained copies of transcripts and other court documents. Then she put together a case history memo, which is a timeline summary of events and facts.

One beautiful day near the beginning of June in 2010, I walked on the yard with Vance. The sun shone in a clear blue sky, the breeze cooled our faces, and we engaged in a stimulating conversation about the Bible.

Suddenly the alarm sounded. The CO in the guard tower shouted, "Everyone lie down in a prone position."

On the yard, an inmate lay in the dirt and his own blood, stabbed to death. The sight and the senseless violence sickened me. Frequent stabbings and slashings left images that remain locked in my mind's eye. No one should ever have to witness a person's lifeblood spraying from the carotid artery.

Although June was marred by that horrible murder, God granted me the best Father's Day I'd ever had. It began with a visit from Mom and Rick. When the visit should have been terminated due to overcrowding, it wasn't. We fed much on Christ that Sunday.

I also fed on meat—real meat. A private kitchen set up at the prison sold a special meal that included steak. This was the first time in over five years that I had eaten my cud-chewing friend from the field. Although it was dry and chewy and lacked flavor, it still tasted amazing.

I anticipated calling Colton that afternoon. But when I returned, I was told there wasn't going to be any program, which usually meant no phone calls. I slumped on my bunk. The beef taste in my mouth turned sour. Colton had been told to expect a call from his daddy. With heaviness radiating from my heart through my whole body, I prayed the Lord would somehow enable me to make that call.

The door opened to reveal the CO. He pointed at me. "You want to make your phone call?"

I hopped off my rack. "Yes, sir. Thank you."

I anxiously dialed the phone number and listened to it ring. Then I heard my little boy's voice. He chatted freely, which was unusual. He answered my questions with great detail. His inquisitiveness and perception astonished me. *What a fine boy the Lord has put in my quiver!*

Colton talked about his leopard gecko, his little friend across the street, and his new home, which he liked. He also told me how much he enjoyed playing outside, which made my heart soar. His mom got on the phone then, but Colton interrupted to tell me about his toads. My fifteen minutes were soon up.

"Goodbye, Colton. I love you. Can we talk again soon?"

"Yes. I love you, too, Daddy."

Colton's interests sounded more and more like mine, which made me both proud and worried. I pleaded with God to develop his praiseworthy attributes and give him strength to resist the temptations I'd too often succumbed to.

One night in September, Jonathan and I watched America's Most Wanted. The program described how a young woman had been attacked, stabbed multiple times, and then left for dead near her mother's home. Miraculously she regained consciousness and crawled to the house, where she called 911. A new detective on the case spoke about testing the victim's shirt for DNA. The attacker had grabbed her from behind, and the detective was "confident" they would find DNA from the perpetrator's sweaty palms.

It was almost as if they were talking about my case. I felt this show was a token from God, telling me to be patient and trust him.

About two months later, my hope burst into bloom when I received a letter from a different law student. Sonia wrote, "Dear Mr. Courtney, I am writing to give you an update on your case. I am happy to report that, as of last week, your case is now considered active in our office."

Those words still fill my soul with joy and my eyes with tears. God had—at last—answered many prayers. The California Innocence Project taking my case validated my truth claim. Someone else at least suspected I had suffered an injustice. Did they know I was innocent? Not yet, but they saw enough evidence to question my conviction.

For many years, I had been without a voice. No one listened and no one cared about what I said. The wings of the wind snatched my professions of innocence and dropped them in the sands of a desert crevice. But the California Innocence Project attorneys and students, whom I call the Agents of Hope, gave voice to the voiceless one. From the distant abyss of Donovan, my voice would be heard in the Superior Court of the State of California in San Diego.

18

Invisible Progression

Richard J. Donovan Correctional Facility, Building 14

Jonathan and I returned to our cell after a sudden and disconcerting strip search. We gasped at the devastation. Bedding had been torn off the racks. Hygiene items and food had been upset or shoved off shelves. Jonathan's evangelistic tracts and our precious books lay scattered over the floor. We stared in numb horror.

Whenever the prison went on lockdown, inmates were searched and cells inspected—often trashed—but this bordered on malicious.

The Squad (a group of COs like internal affairs) entered our cell with a box that measured six cubic feet. A CO set it down. "Put your property in this. Whatever doesn't fit will be sent home or thrown away."

One of the officers stayed to watch us. I immediately began digging through the wreckage to find my most prized books. Most of our worldly possessions posed no problem, but we were allowed only ten books each. And we owned far over the permissible amount.

The CO towered over my short cellmate. Trembling in distress, Jonathan hurried to pick up his tracts. They were his lifeblood, his reason for living. He scurried around, trying to scoop up the flimsy brochures, which tumbled just as quickly from his fluttering hands.

The CO picked up one. "Why do you have so many of these little booklets?" He flustered Jonathan so much that the poor man couldn't even answer coherently.

Finally, I spoke up. "He uses them for his ministry. He mails them out all over the US and the whole world, literally."

The CO shrugged. "Okay. You can keep these things. But the books have to go. You can only have ten."

While he wasn't looking, I stashed a couple of hardcovers that I couldn't part with. Then I offered up a pile of sacrificial lambs.

Jonathan grabbed some of his and handed them to the CO. "Please don't throw them away. I beg you. Could you please donate them to the chapel or something?"

The guard tucked them under his massive arm. "Sure, sure. We'll donate them to the chapel."

The CO finally left us alone, and we attempted to restore order to the chaos. Our shelves looked sparse without the books we'd given up. At least mine got shipped to my parents' house. Jonathan's never showed up in the chapel.

*

That lockdown hit as hard and fast as a tornado and left my mind littered with as much emotional debris. Unfortunately, it was only the beginning of a series of lockdowns that characterized 2011. The entire year seemed like a single prolonged lockdown.

Both 2011 and 2012 were years of continued California Innocence Project involvement in my case, although progress often seemed invisible.

On February 11, 2011, my CIP attorney Alissa Bjerkhoel and a student, Sonia, visited me. Alissa was beautiful and angelic-looking, but I was more struck by her serious and straightforward manner.

I knew they had to stick to the facts, but I felt compelled to tell them, "I'm innocent. I don't know how to prove it to you now, but I believe, Lord willing, you will see that I am telling the truth."

They told me the California Innocence Project had determined there was evidence of innocence and that DNA testing on material evidence would be probative on the issue. We signed a *pro bono* retainer agreement.

The CIP began an extensive writing process, which began with filing a motion for their appointment as counsel. This was a crucial step. Without court appointment, the CIP wouldn't be able to access court documents and evidence. The court initially denied this motion, due to the impression the CIP would seek payment from me. But clients do not pay; the work of the CIP is funded by federal and state grants and private donations.

Once the payment issue was cleared up, the court appointed the California Innocence Project team of Justin Brooks (CIP director), Jan Stiglitz, Alexander Simpson, Alissa Bjerkhoel, and Sarah Bear as my counsel for the purpose of investigating and, if appropriate, preparing a motion for DNA testing.

I had previously filed a motion for DNA testing, which the court rejected without prejudice. Although I'd been devastated at the time, that rejection had been a good thing because now the California Innocence Project could do it and do it right.

Sarah frequently updated me on my case. On January 6, 2012, I received a letter stating that she was in the final stages of completing my motion for DNA testing. She told me it was taking a little more time because she wanted to make sure we put our best foot forward, since the District Attorney's office had not agreed to testing at a previous hearing.

I was astounded. What were they afraid of? If they had been right, the test would prove it. But if not, it would prove my claims of innocence. One person within the DA's office advocated for the DNA testing, but others were not yet of the same mind. Many such roadblocks sprang up throughout my fight for justice and truth.

On February 2, the CIP filed the motion for DNA testing. On February 8, seven years to the day after my arrest in Texas, the court issued an order to show cause and invited the DA's office to respond.

The DA finally agreed that DNA testing in my case was warranted. My attorneys and I cooperated with the DA's office to request that San Diego Superior Court make applicable orders to carry out matters such as: location of evidence, transfer of evidence to the testing facility, testing the evidence and issuing reports, CODIS upload, payment of costs, return of evidence, and hearing date. Baby steps turned into giant strides as my Agents of Hope slashed their way through the treacherous jungle of the justice system.

But it would be months before testing actually began. The evidence needed to be viewed by all the parties involved and then released by the San Diego Superior Court Exhibit Room, but only after it had been packaged in a manner to ensure it would not be damaged during transit, that any potential biological material would be preserved, and that appropriate chain of custody procedures were followed.

In May of 2012, I was unexpectedly called to Committee. I feared I might be moved out of Donovan at this crucial time in my legal process. Since 2011, my points had been low enough for me to be housed on a Level 3 yard, but Donovan didn't have a Level 3 SNY. All these months, I'd been given an override that allowed me to remain on the Level 4 yard, even though I was technically Level 3.

Jonathan and I prayed fervently, asking the Lord to keep us together, or at least keep me from being sent off to another prison. The prison system often arbitrarily ships inmates many miles from families.

But once again the captain and my counselor gave me an override, this time with the likelihood of eventually being endorsed to the Level 3 SNY scheduled to open in the near future at Donovan. Knowing I could remain close to my parents and the CIP for at least another year relieved me to no end.

I'd been under the impression that testing was underway, but was greatly disappointed when I learned in June of 2012 that it hadn't even started. The law enforcement department hadn't sent the SART (sexual assault rape test). Because this department included the detective in my case, I grew paranoid about what might be up. I begged God to preserve the evidence and its integrity.

During a visit on September 1, Mom and Rick told me the lab had finally received all the evidence. Apparently the problem had been mere miscommunication and nothing intentional.

Sarah sent me a letter describing some laboratory procedures. The initial quantification process would determine how much DNA was on a specific piece of evidence. Then the lab would decide the best kind of testing for each item.

Having waited a long time to get to this point, I was both terrified and excited. Everything hinged on the outcome of testing, and the possible scenarios were many. I knew God was able to make the truth known and restore my freedom, but I didn't know if it was his decree to do so. Yet my hope lifted like a balloon on lofty winds.

On October 19, 2012, Alex (my fourth and last law student) and Sarah Bear visited me. They told me that not all the evidence contained testable DNA. About a 50/50 chance existed of something being found on the victim's shirt.

A 50/50 chance? Despair pricked my balloon of hope, and it drifted downward. Sarah and Alex explained different types of testing the lab would conduct, but my mind was so distracted by the poor odds that I found it all confusing.

Weeks went by as I waited to be moved to the new yard and to hear results of the testing. My adrenaline long since exhausted, I felt like a depleted robot, waiting for my master to install a new battery and set me going again.

On the evening of December 7, I received a letter from Alex (dated December 5), which said they had received some preliminary results from the DNA testing. This initial information indicated male DNA on the victim's shirt, but excluded me as a contributor.

Obviously, this was very good news indeed. My DNA was not on the victim's shirt, as I knew it wouldn't be. But this was only the first hurdle in an obstacle course of legal barriers. And I'd face the rest of my race without my buddy Jonathan.

19

Full Circle

Richard J. Donovan Correctional Facility, D Yard

I paced across the cell one more time.

Jonathan paused in his prayers. "You've been a good cellie, Uriah."

"You, too, brother." The lump in my throat threatened to choke me. We'd said similar goodbyes to each other over and over for the last two days. Two nights earlier, a CO had told me I'd be moved in the morning. But I hadn't been moved the next morning or the one after that.

By this time, I felt like a watch that had been wound too tightly.

A CO came to the cell door, and he had a garbage buggy with him. "Courtney, you're moving out."

I quickly bagged up the few items of property that I'd been using the last two days, and put all my sacks of personal possessions in the buggy. Jonathan and I said our final goodbyes while the CO waited by the door.

With the CO ambling beside me, I pushed the buggy all the way to D Yard. But when we arrived, the staff didn't even know what building I was going to. I hung around for an hour or so, before being escorted back to C Yard.

Pushing the buggy back over the same terrain, I tried to keep my anger in check. A CO came out of Central Control, and waved a paper. "Courtney, I have your bed move order."

I stopped. "Yeah? Where to?"

"D Yard. Building 20."

I sighed and maneuvered the awkward buggy around. That was the last numbered building in the entire complex.

As I settled in my new cell, I reflected on my location. This building was closest to the exit and next to the visiting room I'd first used at Donovan, so many years earlier. It seemed I had come full circle.

I started out in Receiving and Release, but was put in CTC, located in the middle of the grounds. Then I had been taken to B Yard and put in Ad-Seg in Building 7 until I went to Committee. Eventually I was released from the hole and sent to Building 9 on the Reception yard. After a very long time in Reception, I was moved to C Yard, first Building 13, then 15, and then 14. And now I was on D Yard, in Building 20. I had lived in three out of the four prison yards and resided in seven different buildings.

My full-circle progress was most apparent when Mom and Rick visited me, in the same place that had been our initial visiting room at Donovan. Only it had undergone radical changes. Then we'd peered at each other through thick glass and tried to talk through broken telephones. Now all those cubicle walls had been ripped out, and we sat together at a table, speaking face to face.

I smiled at Mom. "Can you believe we're sitting here? In the very room where we had our first visit?"

Mom wiped a tear. "I felt so angry and helpless, seeing you here in prison, sentenced to life for a crime you didn't commit."

"Let's not talk about that now." Rick patted her arm. Then he pointed up. "Hey, Uriah, take a look at the ceiling. I'd never let you guys get by with that."

The crew hadn't finished the job very well. The outlines where the walls had been still showed on the ceiling.

"I know. You're pickier than that." I pointed down. "You'd think they'd at least have filled in the spaces with tile." Bare cement floor showed through where every wall had stood.

"What poor workmanship." Rick shook his head. "They probably figured, who cares? It's just a prison visiting room."

We chuckled.

"Sure looks different than last time we were here." I leaned back in my chair and glanced around at the open area dotted with tables. "I feel different now, too. More comfortable."

Mom nodded. "I feel the same way."

"God has had a hand in this," Rick said. "Think about it, Uriah. You've gone from this room to the depths of the back of the prison, then returned to where we started." He pointed to the windows. "From here, you can see the gates you'll walk out one day."

Later Rick suggested we go outside to visit on the patio, which was surrounded by tall block walls, but open to the sky. While we were there, someone took a picture of the three of us.

Rick gripped my shoulder. "This is the last photo we'll take in prison."

*

I hoped Rick was right. Level 3 may have had more privileges, but the new yard was still ironing out the program schedules. And I remained on a high custody status. I often sat in my little prison cell, staring at the wall and wondering if these gray blocks would be the last thing I'd see before I died.

In January of 2013, I received a letter from Alex, telling me that additional lab results excluded me as a contributor to the male portion of the DNA on the victim's shirt and skirt. The lab discovered male DNA on the victim's clothing exactly where she testified her attacker grabbed her. The DNA was first compared to mine and, of course, it didn't match.

Those results may have been sufficient for a new trial someday, but they weren't enough to exonerate. What I needed was a match to the male profile they found. The CIP was coordinating with the lab to send the electronic data from the DNA testing to the Orange County Crime Lab for a possible CODIS (combined DNA index system) upload.

Why Orange County when the crime took place in San Diego County? It was because both San Diego County and Los Angeles County authorities had refused to upload the profile. One has to wonder about those refusals. It demonstrates a systematic lack of cooperation from many DAs and law enforcement agencies with innocence organizations across the country, which makes their work much more difficult, although inroads are being made.

The Orange County Crime Lab agreed to upload the data into CODIS only if they determined there was enough DNA to form an appropriate profile. And discovering if there was sufficient data could be determined only if they actually uploaded it.

So even at this point, uncertainty loomed over me. In the event we were unable to upload the data into CODIS, I was informed there would be other options for me to pursue.

I knew of nothing to do other than pray, which I certainly did. As difficult and stressful as this time was, I remember feeling very close to God. It seems God uses our greatest tribulations to help us realize how utterly dependent we are on his fatherly care. I had no recourse but to ask, seek, knock. My entire being prostrated itself before the throne on high.

Proverbs 21:1 says, "The king's heart is a stream of water in the hand of the Lord; he turns it wherever he will." I knew only God could move the hearts of those in charge of the Orange County Crime Lab to see that the data was appropriate, or God could make the data sufficient and get it uploaded. And I prayed fervently for God to act.

20

Amazing Days

Richard J. Donovan Correctional Facility, D Yard

About 12:30 in the afternoon on February 1, 2013, I was unexpectedly called out and escorted to the visiting center.

Inside the building, a CO met me. "There's a bunch of people here to see you."

"What's it about?"

He shrugged. "Don't know. Kinda curious myself. Sure you don't know what's up?"

I shook my head. "I have no idea." Heartbeats hammered my ribs so hard I found it difficult to breathe. "Do you know who they are?"

"No." He grinned. "Except they're attorneys and three of them are very pretty ladies."

The CIP!

He led me to the attorney-client visiting room and opened the door.

I was surprised to see four faces looking up at me. A man I recognized as Justin Brooks sat with Sarah, Alissa, and Alex. They all quickly stood, and Justin shook my hand. "Hello, Uriah. I'm Justin Brooks."

"Yes, I know. I've seen you on TV." Laughter rippled around the room.

"Uriah, there are only two reasons why I'd be here." He held up a finger. "One is that we have very bad news, or two"—he put up another finger—"we have very good news." He smiled. "Congratulations, Uriah. We have very good news."

I dropped into a chair and broke down.

For the first time in years, tears poured from my eyes. I didn't like even these people seeing me cry, so I buried my face in my arms on the table. Tears rolled down my cheeks, over my arms, and onto the table.

When I looked up, the others sat around me, smiling through their own tears. This was an amazing day for them, too. They had fought the good fight and saved the life of their client.

Alissa wiped mascara from her cheek. "The DNA collected from the victim's clothing was uploaded into CODIS and they found a match."

I whispered, "Praise God."

"You know, Uriah," Justin said, "the DA's office is doing an investigation into the guy, so they won't tell us who he is. What I can tell you, however, is that he was arrested for similar sexual offenses multiple times and ended up in the database."

Alissa spoke up. "The thing is, Uriah, this guy looks just like you and he lived nearby."

I touched my chest. "This creep looks like me?"

She nodded.

Alex said, "The actual perpetrator and you do look alike."

No one said anything for a minute, and I tried to process what I'd heard. My thoughts spun. *Just think. If they'd found him in November of 2004, maybe, just maybe, there wouldn't be other victims out there now.*

Alissa reached over to touch my hand. "The important thing is that the match definitively clears you."

"That's right, Uriah." Justin grasped my shoulder and shook it. "These things take time, but we're going to do our best to get you out of here as soon as possible."

As I looked around the room, every face beamed. They had worked hard on my case in a team effort, but Alissa's face shone. In her look, I saw compassion and conviction, strength and courage. I was her client and this was the fruit of her diligent labors.

"We need to caution you about one thing." Justin leaned close. "You can't tell anyone."

My eyebrows shot up. "Not even my parents?"

"Not even them."

"Why not?"

Justin cleared his throat. "Some important matters still need to be worked out between the CIP and the DA's office regarding your release, and we don't want the media catching wind of things just yet and creating a commotion."

"Hey," I shrugged, "I know I'm going home soon, so no big deal. I can keep my mouth shut."

Alissa said, "You know, I don't think it will happen, Uriah, but the worst-case scenario would be if the DA contested the findings. Then we'd have to go out and litigate."

"Another trial?" I was horrified. "That's absolutely ridiculous!"

"Yes, it is. But it's a very real possibility."

They shared some potential options that could be implemented should the DA decide to contest. Then we all stood and embraced.

Alissa stepped back from me, smiling. "We'll be in touch again very soon."

As I left the visiting center, I quite literally felt like I was walking on clouds. Everything had an entirely different feel to it. My senses seemed keener than in years. The sky gleamed a more vivid blue, the sun glowed more brightly, and the mountains loomed more immensely. Even the COs and other inmates seemed less threatening. I was innocent, and everyone would soon know it.

*

For the remainder of the day and far into the night, I mused about how this wonderful news arrived exactly a week before the anniversary of my arrest on February 8, 2005. For nearly eight years, I'd prayed for my exoneration and that day had finally come. This would be an extremely difficult secret to keep from my parents. I imagined the look on my mom's face when I told her. How precious that would be!

The very next day Rick and Mom visited. Before we sat down, I gave Mom an extra long hug. After years of suppressing my emotions, it was easy to control my outward appearance. But inside was an entirely different story.

During the first ten or fifteen minutes of our conversation, I must have decided to tell them and then decided against it about a thousand times. No longer able to contain my joy, I felt I must share this good news. They had done all this time right along with me and they deserved to know.

I took a deep breath. "You wanna go outside for a while?"

They were surprised, because I'd never suggested this before. We walked onto the patio, where Rick and I sat on one of the benches. Mom stood in front of me, and I couldn't keep the grin off my face.

I grabbed her hand and looked into her eyes. "Mom, I'm coming home."

She stared and leaned closer. "What? What did you say?"

"They ran the DNA profile through CODIS and they got a match. I'm coming home."

"Oh, my God." She began to sob. "Thank you, God."

I stood and embraced her. Rick threw his arms around both of us. "That's awesome, Uriah!"

Their faces glistened with tears and glowed with joy.

While they struggled to regain their composure, I shared what the CIP had told me and what might happen now. Too excited to sit still, Mom paced in front of Rick and me the entire time I talked.

All too soon, our visit ended. I hugged them again. "I'll let the CIP know that I've told you about this, and tell them they may communicate with you about what's going on. But you must swear not to tell another soul."

Mom nodded. "I understand, Uriah. If we tell our friends and family, they'll be so thrilled the news will spread like wildfire."

Rick patted my shoulder. "We promise. We'll sit tight on it."

I can't adequately describe my emotions during those days of joy-filled secrecy. I had gone from not knowing if I'd ever taste and see freedom again, to knowing that my restored liberty was not a mere morsel of hope but a certainty. I experienced unbridled happiness so sweet I almost felt as if I had been physically born again. I knew it was only the beginning of the joy set before me. The continual delight began slowly washing away my pain.

I had often dreamed of the day when I could say, "You meant it for evil, but God meant it for good." It had taken years for that verse in Genesis 50 to really sink in, and I finally was able to see it in a whole new light. I had resisted the idea that any good could come from this, but it surely had. And I knew God would be glorified.

Alissa, Sarah, and Alex came to give me a progress report later in February. At that time, they were finding it difficult to persuade everyone in the DA's office to accept the facts. They also shared that the state of Nevada wanted me back. I wasn't terribly surprised about either of these developments, but I hoped a statute of limitations would run out or Nevada would simply let me be. I just wanted to be free again and left alone.

To handle my court hearing in Nevada, the CIP provided me with an attorney named Raquel Cohen, who was licensed to practice law in both

California and Nevada. I was under the impression Nevada authorities would pick me up from Donovan and extradite me to Nye County.

We all hoped the judge there would show mercy after learning of my wrongful conviction and incarceration. If not, I faced another six to twelve months in a Nevada jail or prison. What a dreadful thought!

Uriah, I told myself, *you can do that standing on your head if that's what it comes to. You'll have a definite date of release, and that's all that matters.*

Of course, I didn't want to be incarcerated for another day, but I was willing to accept the consequences of my actions. The repentant sinner still must answer for his sins in the eyes of the law here and now. God forgives, but the justice system doesn't.

In March, Sarah and Alex paid me another visit. The DA's office had come to some kind of agreement with the CIP for my release. Sarah and Alex didn't share the details, but they told me the DA's office had up to 180 days after my release to decide whether to retry the case.

I stared at them in horror. "That can still happen? I could go to trial again, even after I've been out for six months?"

Sarah said, "With everything in your favor, especially the DNA test, the likelihood of that happening is very slim."

Alex nodded. "It would be a foolish waste of time and money on the DA's part."

I couldn't believe I might have to live through the hell of a trial again, but I tried not to dwell on that as I began to anticipate my release. I sorted through my worldly possessions, deciding what to keep and send home with my parents or what I'd give away.

I gave away many things to brothers in the Lord who had no outside support. I boxed up my precious study books and Bible to send home. After they were gone, I lay in bed and gazed at the empty shelf with a deep sense of loneliness. Not having them in view and within reach grieved me. Those books had been my faithful companions, my bosom buddies, for what seemed a lifetime. I reminded myself with prayerful confidence that I'd see them again very soon, on a shelf in my own room at my parents' house.

It was only during this memoir-writing process that I realized how God had replaced the close attachment and affection I once felt for drugs and alcohol with intimacy for theology and his Word.

Initially few inmates knew about my exoneration, primarily for safety reasons. It may come as a surprise, but inmates can be viciously jealous and cause trouble for someone going home. Only a few days before I left, the D Yard pastor asked me to give my testimony at chapel.

I clutched the podium and looked at the many staring faces. The place was packed. I spoke about how drug and alcohol abuse nearly destroyed my life, admitting that had I not been locked up when I was, I'd probably be dead. I shared how I was born again in county jail, and how difficult the process of sanctification proved to be. Without going into specifics, I said that I had been wrongfully convicted eight years ago and now had been exonerated through DNA testing with the help of the California Innocence Project. I concluded, "This whole experience has been for God's glory."

Many men talked to me afterward, wishing me well and praising God. Later, my cellie told me he'd noticed some guys wiping tears from their eyes.

On April 13, 2013, Alex and Alissa visited. The entire staff at CIP was bursting with joy, and they wanted to share that with me. They also said I should be transferred any day now, but they didn't know exactly when.

As excited as I was to be going home, I was nervous and scared. Nothing was the same, and it never would be. I was a new creation, but I had also been somewhat institutionalized and certainly traumatized. I didn't know what to expect. Alissa shared some helpful stories about what other exonerees had experienced when they got out. We hugged for the last time in that place.

About forty-five minutes after they left, two of my regular floor officers told me they'd received a phone call that I would be transferred on April 15. They didn't know where, but I assumed Nevada would pick me up.

The next day, April 14, my parents visited and relayed information from Alissa that the San Diego Sheriff's Department would transfer me back to San Diego County Jail (SDCJ) for an extradition hearing.

I don't remember much about this visit because my mind was so overwhelmed with excitement and joy. I do recall, however, eating a very tasty *carne asada* burrito for lunch. Also, for the first time our goodbye hugs weren't sad, but filled with anticipation about the hugs we'd soon share in the free world.

On my last night in Donovan, I prepared a huge spread for my cellie and myself: burritos with refried beans, ramen noodles, rice, tuna, and some crushed cheese crackers for cheesiness. What a feast! I doubted I would be able to sleep, but I did. I even slept well.

The next morning, April 15, 2013, on the way out for breakfast, a CO stopped me. "Uriah, you'll be going over to Receiving and Release shortly."

I went ahead to the chow hall and found my friend Robert. "Hey, Robert. I'm leaving this morning."

He hugged me. "That's great, Uriah. Stay in touch, will ya?"

Too excited to eat, I gave away my breakfast, but I did keep a couple of things out of my lunch sack to munch on later, so I wouldn't get nauseated.

As soon as I returned to my building, the CO motioned to me. "Courtney, grab your property and walk over to the D Yard gate. Wait there for an officer to take you over to R & R."

I picked up my bundle, said *adios* to my cellie, and paused at a few other cell doors to say goodbye to some inmates I considered friends. Everyone was excited and happy for me. Not one person that morning or for days prior to my release showed me the least bit of disrespect. God's protective hedge was impenetrable all those years. He had allowed only a few thorns in the flesh to humble, chasten, and train me.

I stood at the gate for a long time, watching inmates come and go for breakfast. A number of guys I knew asked where I was going.

Each time I answered with a grin, "Going home!"

They all wished me well. Most of them said, "Good luck."

And I always responded, "Not good luck, but good providence."

At last, a CO I had known for years came over to the gate. He had always treated me respectfully, and this was no exception. He grinned. "Big day, isn't it?"

I nodded. "Sure is."

"If you ever make it to my church, and we see each other, I'd be happy to shake your hand and buy you a burger."

"Thanks! That would be great. And thank you for your kindness all these years."

As he walked me across the plaza to R & R, I gazed around. Here I was—leaving a yard gate for the last time. Whenever I'd picked up a package from R & R, I'd always thought it was the place where other inmates got released, but not me—I was a lifer.

But here I am.

In R & R, I paced in a holding tank for a couple of hours, praying and reciting Scripture. My thoughts raced as I attempted to process things. I would be transferred to San Diego County Jail (SDCJ). I would go back to Nevada to answer for an old warrant. And I'd soon be going home—maybe in a matter of days, weeks, or months—but no more than a year.

I heard new voices outside the cell and peered through the tiny window. There they were. Two sheriff's deputies. My name was mentioned. A few seconds later, a CO walked over and unlocked the door. I was instructed to remove my prison blues and go through the usual routine.

That business done, the deputies handed me the familiar county jail outfit. After I put it on, they clamped irons around my ankles and wrists and shackled the chains to my waist. The cuffs weren't too tight, and I was absolutely delighted to be finally on my way.

They loaded me into a white van with a built-in cage in the back. I took my seat, and they even buckled the seat belt for me. We paused at the main security gate, where they showed my transfer papers to a CO, and we went on. Then we stopped at a small building for the deputies to retrieve their weapons. One more gate to go.

We passed through. That was it. I was outside the prison grounds.

As we drove away, I looked back at the place of my captivity.

Thank you, Lord, that I'm leaving it for good.

21

Release Odyssey

San Diego County Jail and Nevada

Despite being shackled during the ride to San Diego County Jail, I felt euphoric. The van seemed a carriage and the deputies my coachmen. My shackles became golden chains, my wrist and ankle cuffs turned to bracelets festooned with precious gems. The security mesh covering the windows was but a silk screen to ward off the sun's bright beams.

Five years ago, I'd traveled this same freeway in a massive bus, shackled to another inmate, not knowing if I'd ever see sunlight outside a prison wall again. Now I traveled the opposite direction, away from prison and toward eventual freedom.

The van passed the road leading to my parents' home, only five minutes away. *Soon I'll be riding down that road as a free man.*

Trees and buildings whizzed past as if I were in a racecar. Every color and object flashed by in vivid detail, overstimulating my senses, while a mixture of distress and exhilaration coursed through my body.

*

The van passed through the immense steel gate of SDCJ and entered the concrete structure below the jail. The door slid open, and a deputy unbuckled my seatbelt and helped me step down. The familiar musty, exhaust-steeped air assaulted me. Choking fumes filled my throat, as distressing memories flooded my mind. Arrests for drug and alcohol violations fluttered before my internal eyes like a slide show. But the images stopped at my extradition from Texas to San Diego, when I'd been clueless to my future.

The reality of my rebellious, wasted years weighed me down. I hoped the Lord would use the sting of my past sins, like a schoolmaster's stern rebuke, to keep me from temptation.

In the processing area, I bypassed some routine booking procedures but was shuffled between holding tanks to see a nurse and a psych doctor. Eventually I was placed in a fairly large tank and told to wait while they found housing for me. Surprisingly, I was alone during the entire process, and the place was eerily quiet and devoid of activity.

Some time later, a deputy opened the slot in the door and handed me a brown paper bag containing an orange, two slices of bread, and a thin strip of unknown meat. Because I'd eaten hardly anything for breakfast, that meager lunch did little to dispel my hunger.

Minutes became hours, and I grew tired and restless. The cell was cold, and I was bored. I paced back and forth, praying and wishing I had my Bible. It lay with my few other personal possessions in a large paper bag directly outside the holding tank.

A deputy walked by.

"Sir," I called through the slot. "Could I please have my Bible? It's right there in that bag on the floor."

He shook his head. "No. Sorry." His footsteps echoed away.

It was the answer I'd expected, but not the one I'd hoped for. I continued pacing, reciting Scripture from memory.

Much later, another deputy approached.

"Hey, sir." I called again through the slot. "Could you please hand me my Bible? It's in the bag lying right there."

"No. You can't have personal property in booking." He walked on.

I continued pacing, praying with the Lord's Prayer as a paradigm. Many fearful, hopeful, and joyful musings flitted through my mind, and I poured it all before the Lord.

In the middle of a sentence, I glanced up and recognized two smiling faces on the other side of the tempered glass window. The Budloves!

We moved to the crevice between the door and the cinder block wall, where we could hear each other better.

"Greetings in the Lord." Pastor Budlove's voice warmed my heart.

Mom Budlove's smile conveyed her love. "It's so good to see you again, Uriah."

"It's terrific to see you again, too." I grinned through the glass. "Did you hear that I'll be exonerated of the charges for my life sentence?"

"Praise God for that," they exclaimed with delight. "Your parents told us you were being moved today. That's why we're here."

After a joyous conversation, Pastor Budlove prayed, thanking God for answering the prayers of many and allowing me my day in court to reveal the truth.

The warm glow from the Budloves' visit helped me get through the monotony of my remaining hours in the holding tank, broken only by a meal that reminded me of the worst kind of TV dinner.

At 9:00 p.m,, after I'd been in booking for almost twelve hours, a deputy opened my door. He handed me the bag containing my belongings, and I was taken to Floor 7.

That was the very same floor I'd been on when first extradited from Texas. Not only had I gone full circle at Donovan, but it seemed I also was going back to the beginning in county jail.

The next day I was escorted to the courthouse for my extradition hearing. The holding area is a maze of narrow hallways and small tanks. But I was placed at the front of this section, in a cell with old-style bars from floor to ceiling. It was one of the few spots that allowed me to see people walking by.

As I stood looking out, a familiar form approached. It was the bailiff who had witnessed my entire trial. He recognized me, too, and walked over. "How are you doing, Uriah?"

"Actually, I'm doing pretty well. The California Innocence Project took on my case. They were able to get new DNA testing done on the victim's clothes."

"Really?"

"Yes. The test results were run through CODIS and matched a registered sex offender, so I'll be completely exonerated of the crime."

"Oh, that's great news."

"I was telling the truth. I'm innocent."

He shook his head. "I always felt things weren't right with that case."

"That's an understatement."

"So what are you doing back here?"

"I have to be extradited to Nevada to clear up an outstanding warrant. I won't get more than a year, but I hope the judge will be lenient."

"I hope so, too." He smiled. "Congratulations and best of luck to you."

How liberating to assure the man who saw it all that I truly was innocent!

Justin and Alissa represented me at the hearing. When I entered the courtroom, Alex sat in the audience. She smiled and waved.

The hearing was short and cordial. My attorneys presented the facts about the post-conviction DNA testing. The parties involved agreed I should be released from custody on my own recognizance until the District Attorney's office had time to consider all the evidence and proceed appropriately. But both parties also acknowledged that the warrant from Nye County in Nevada prevented me from being released at that time.

As I stood next to my attorneys after the proceedings, Deputy DA Brent Neck walked over and looked in my eyes. "Good luck, Uriah."

"Thanks." His kindness touched me, and I appreciated his cooperation with the CIP in my case.

Mom and Rick visited the next day in the familiar room we'd used years before. Despite those old, broken phones and the thick, tempered glass, we were excited and hopeful, eager to proclaim my innocence to the whole world.

The surreal experience of sitting in that same room caused me to reflect on how this was the jail system where I'd lived through the relentless trauma of my trial. But also where I'd come to know the Lord.

During those initial days, I'd been on fire for Christ. When that feeling waned, I felt like an empty and broken vessel. Until the Lord filled the void and sealed the cracks with sound biblical knowledge. Then he refined those repairs by sending me through the furnace of affliction.

Peter's words came to mind: "In this you rejoice, though now for a little while, if necessary, you have been grieved by various trials, so that the tested genuineness of your faith—more precious than gold that perishes though it is tested by fire—may be found to result in praise and glory and honor at the revelation of Jesus Christ" (1 Pet 1:6–7).

How those words now seemed to apply to me! I hoped and prayed that God would be glorified in my present life as well as when Christ returned.

A few days later, I was escorted down to a holding tank early in the morning. I wondered how I'd be taken to Nevada. It was only an hour flight from San Diego to Las Vegas, so I hoped it would be by plane.

After an hour's wait, a deputy and two uniformed men approached. Because US Marshals had originally extradited me, I'd assumed they would do it again. But I didn't recognize the logo or name of the private security firm on these uniforms.

As they escorted me down the hall, I asked, "Will we be flying to Nevada?"

They replied, "No."

My spirits plummeted. It would be a long drive to Pahrump, shackled in the back of a van.

When we entered the musty underground garage, my spirits sank lower. The transport vehicle had a van front, but the back was a specially designed box with no side windows—only a sliver in the back door.

They opened the cage. A man sat on a narrow ledge along one side. My chains rattling, I greeted him and climbed inside. I sat opposite him on an identical shelf, about twelve inches deep and six feet long. A couple of filthy pillows lay between our feet. The box door closed and its lock clicked.

I sighed. "This is going to be a long ride in such a small space."

"Sure is." He nodded in the dim light. "Where you going?"

"Pahrump. Just outside Las Vegas."

"I'm going to Carson City."

"Oh, man. You've got a really long ride ahead of you."

We pulled out of the garage. Through the tiny window, I watched the huge steel gate swing shut behind us. I silently praised God for bringing me out of that terrible place for the last time.

As we headed north on Interstate 15, I peered out in amazement. So many things had changed! New buildings, houses, apartments, and streets had sprung up. We passed the city where Misty lived, but it had grown so much that it hardly looked like the same place.

We stopped to pick up an inmate at another jail, where we were permitted to use the restroom. When we returned to our shelves in the box, we three inmates conversed for a while but then fell silent.

My thoughts churned. Going back to Pahrump seemed like such a waste. *Hasn't the system taken plenty from me already? Haven't they squandered enough time and money by wrongfully convicting me?*

I knew I had to answer for breaking the law and violating probation, but I desperately wanted to get out and begin my new life.

At least these guys drive fast. My heart raced. *What if a tire blows? Or we have a collision at this high rate of speed? We have no seat belts. We'll be tossed around like rag dolls in this can.*

I pushed away those vivid and disturbing images with prayer, asking the Lord to see that we all arrived safely at our destinations.

We stopped at a McDonalds, where we were permitted to relieve ourselves again. People stared at the three men in jumpsuits, shackled together and guarded by two uniformed men with firearms strapped to their hips. One of the guards gave each of us two mini burritos, which I scarfed down.

After another hour and a half, we arrived in Las Vegas. It had definitely grown in the ten years since I'd been there. A stop at the infamous Clark County Detention Facility provided another bathroom break. Considering my previous life, I could easily have been in that jail before, but it was my first glimpse inside.

Then we drove to a parking area on the northern outskirts, where we switched vehicles and escorts, boarding a van with seats and belts. I asked the new drivers, "Are we going to Pahrump now?"

One shook his head. "We won't stop in Pahrump but will drop you off in Tonopah."

"Tonopah? I'm supposed to go to Pahrump. Why are you taking me way up there?"

"Because that's what our paperwork says."

Unbelievable. My stomach knotted. We were only an hour from Pahrump, but they were taking me more than three hours north to Tonopah.

I wondered if God was showing me all the jails I could have ended up in, but hadn't because he had prevented it.

We drove through one rundown little desert town after another. At last, we pulled into the sally port at Tonopah. It was 5:00 p.m. and we'd been on the road since 7:00 a.m.

A Nye County Sheriff's deputy handled my booking process. My paperwork stated: Outstanding Warrant for PERFORMANCE OF AN ACT OR NEGLECT OF DUTY IN WILLFUL OR WANTON DISREGARD OF SAFETY OR PERSON OR PROPERTY. Sentence: 1 YEAR NYE COUNTY JAIL.

I'd known what I potentially faced, but to actually see it screaming on paper disheartened me. I donned a white and bright orange striped jail outfit and was put inside a holding tank.

A few minutes later, the deputy came back with a roll of toilet paper and a blanket. He said it was too late for dinner but offered to bring me something. He soon returned with a sandwich and some chips.

As I ate, I sat on the bunk and looked around. It was a bit different from other cells I'd been in, but it had one thing in common with them. I couldn't leave of my own volition.

A couple of hours later, the deputy came back and opened the door. "Follow me."

"Before we leave the booking area," I asked, "could I please have my Bible out of my property bag?"

He granted my request. My hands closed around my small ESV, and I took a deep breath. Now that I had my sword and lamp, I felt more at ease.

My assigned cell was on the top tier, and I had it all to myself. Tonopah was entirely different from what I was accustomed to. Race or gang drama seemed nonexistent, and there was no shot caller checking paperwork. The other inmates appeared to be either alcohol or drug addicts. This was the calmest jail in my experience. I decided to shower.

Washing away traveling grime felt wonderful, but before I'd finished, the deputy in the "fish tank" (control booth) announced that dayroom was now closed. I quickly rinsed and returned to my cell while still half wet.

I made my bed and sat on it, thoughts flitting through my mind like a squawking flock of messy sparrows. Regardless of what happened in court, at least I would be given a release date.

Today is Dad's birthday. I felt bad about not calling him, but I assumed he'd been informed about my extradition to Nevada. He'd be relieved to know that this terrible injustice would soon be over.

The following day I called him as well as Mom and Rick. I also spoke to Colton. I felt far away from everyone, but Mom and Rick assured me they'd be present for my court date.

Later, a probation officer visited me. She told me the outcome was entirely up to the judge. I shared how my experience had dramatically changed my life and that I intended to cooperate completely with the court. I expressed my hope for a second opportunity to be placed on probation and my desire to return to California and live with my mom and stepdad. Her subsequent report of our exchange was unbiased and fair.

On April 24, I was transferred to Pahrump. I stepped into the bright sunshine and blinked in surprise. A new building stood before me. The old building, which had been fabricated by welding together large sections of an old ship, was now used as a juvenile detention facility.

Like booking processes in California, this one turned out to be an all-day affair. Late that evening, my name was finally called and I was led through the shiny, new building. It seemed a large jail for a town of only 30,000 people. And almost all of the cells appeared occupied.

All eyes turned toward me as I walked in and carried my bedroll up the stairs. This crowd looked more like the ones in California: the grizzled biker, the tattooed skinhead, and the Mexican gangbanger. What a relief to no longer worry about someone questioning my paperwork!

After settling in, I headed downstairs to mingle and discovered a lack of politics. Another huge relief. The main topic of discussion was that the new jail was disorganized and understaffed, which meant fewer privileges.

I returned to my cell and tried to calm my nerves. I had been hell on wheels in Pahrump, and many of those past debaucheries rushed back. Things I'd forgotten and many I hadn't seemed as fresh as yesterday. As the images played before my mind's eye, shame and remorse filled my heart. I'd repented of these sins long ago, but now their memory cast a dark cloud on my soul. I knew Satan wanted to prevent me from having peace. I reminded myself that, despite my poor choices in Pahrump, I had learned a lot and experienced some good things there.

I phoned Mom, Dad, or Colton every day. Because the dayroom area was small and cramped, my only exercise was walking up and down the stairs. My whole being was so taut I longed to scale the walls and bust out. *Stand on my head for a year in this tiny pit? No way.*

Reading Scripture helped fix my mind on God's sovereignty. My entire time in jail and prison had been a testament to the truth, and it would be no different here. God knew I wanted to get baptized and become a member of a sound, Bible-believing church. He knew my desire to serve and magnify him. My chief prayer had long been for my exoneration and God's glory.

The two would go hand in hand, but I knew his glory was not contingent upon my exoneration. God had led me through my treacherous hell, and I was eager to tell the world how he got me through it and turned evil to good. I prayerfully hoped God was ready to be publicly glorified in my exoneration now—not in six or twelve months.

My court date was set for May 6, 2013. Mom and Rick as well as CIP attorneys Alex Simpson and Raquel Cohen planned to arrive on May 5.

I learned from guys in my module that the judge could go either way, harsh or lenient. On May 5, I wrote a letter to him.

Your Honor,

The time I spent in prison with a life sentence hanging over my head was a life-changing experience. It caused me to reflect on my life and how I had wasted it and hurt the people I loved most. I saw the error of my ways and decided if I didn't do something about it now, then I never would. You see, I had hope and faith in God that some day I would be exonerated of my wrongful conviction and, if given a second opportunity at life, I wouldn't want to waste it ever again.

I've been clean and sober now for eight years. I've also been a born-again Christian for that long, and it's because of my faith in Christ and the strength he's given me that I've been able to maintain my sobriety and not lose hope during these extremely challenging years of my incarceration. That being said, Your Honor, with respect to my continued sobriety when my freedom is restored to me, I never want to return to jail or prison again, nor hurt or disappoint my family, especially my son, and of course my parents who have done all this time right along with me. I also have many goals that I want to accomplish. I know what I must do in order to see these things come to fruition, and I know what I must not do in order for me to stay out of jail and prison. Clean living. Staying clean and sober is a choice, and it's one that I made eight years ago.

Your Honor, when you make your decision whether or not to allow me to go home with my parents today, I ask for your mercy and that you would please take into consideration the traumatizing experience I've been through, the time I've already served, and the fact that people such as myself really can turn their lives around for the better.

Uriah Courtney

The next day my name was called for court. A couple of deputies collected inmates and escorted us out the jail and up a ramp into holding tanks in the back of the courthouse.

I was nervous, but nothing compared to earlier hearings. While other inmates bantered or argued, I communed silently with the Lord. I prayed passionately that today would be his appointed time for my release.

"Courtney." A deputy stood by the door.

"Yes." I walked forward.

"Let's go." He led me to the courtroom. Alex and Raquel sat at the defense table. He all-business and stern. She beautiful and smartly dressed. They looked like a great team.

Mom and Rick sat behind them. Their faces lit up and they waved. Handcuffs prevented me from waving back, but I smiled and nodded.

Court was called into session. My attorneys admitted the outstanding warrant and my responsibility for it. They then described my wrongful conviction and DNA exoneration.

The prosecuting attorney acknowledged my experience, but argued that I still needed to answer for the warrant. He requested that I remain in custody and serve one year in jail.

The judge asked my attorneys some questions. They mentioned that my parents had come from San Diego with the hope of taking me home.

Alex stood. "Your Honor, Mr. Courtney has written a letter to you, if you'd like to read it."

The judge affirmed that he would, and the bailiff handed it to him. He read and then laid down the paper. He made some comments to the DA.

Then he looked out at the courtroom. "I believe Mr. Courtney has served his time. The court declares Uriah Courtney be released from custody."

My mom gasped with relief. A sudden giddiness surged through my body, and my muscles went limp.

The judge gave me strict orders to check into the probation department before leaving town. I turned to look at Mom and Rick, their faces shining with smiles and tears.

Raquel and Alex said they'd wait for me with my parents in the jailhouse lobby.

"Thanks." My smile widened. "See you soon."

I floated after the bailiff out of the courtroom. I was so filled with joyful excitement and caught up with thanksgiving and praise to God, I can't remember the walk back to jail. I do recall entering the module, where a few guys asked how it went.

I smiled. "I'm going home." What sweet and precious words!

The inmates congratulated me, but I wanted to be alone with the Lord. I headed upstairs and sat on the bunk.

Thank you, Father God. Thank you for getting me through this entire experience. Thank you for letting me go home at last.

It was between 10:30 and 11:00 a.m. when I returned from court, and I didn't expect I'd be released until after noon. I ate lunch, but was restless. The clock became a menace as I watched the hours slowly creep by. I read in my cell, paced in the cramped dayroom, or glanced at the Discovery program others watched on TV. But I couldn't sit still for more than a few minutes. The synapses in my brain fired off faster than the speed of light, and every fiber of my being wanted to move.

Finally it was 5:00 p.m. I was hungry again but ate only part of my dinner and gave away the rest.

What are Mom, Rick, Alex, and Raquel doing? Have they been waiting out there since this morning? Or were they able to find out my release time?

None of the deputies could give me any information. *Why haven't I been taken out and processed for release?* I consoled myself with the knowledge that I was, indeed, getting out. *Just try to be patient.*

"Courtney, grab your things and come to the gate."

"Yes!" I punched the air and picked up my stuff.

Some of the guys called out, "Take care," or "Good luck to you."

The deputy took me to a holding tank in the booking area. A few minutes later, he returned and handed me my property bag containing the belongings I'd brought from San Diego. Except for my Bible, I hadn't seen any of them since I'd left county jail.

The deputy closed the door, although he didn't lock it. "Get dressed and come out when you're done."

I grabbed gray shorts and white running shoes out of my bag and quickly put them on. I walked out of the tank.

The deputy looked up. "Where's your shirt?"

"I don't have one."

He finished the paperwork and asked me to sign a form. "Okay, that's it." He led me over to a large steel door and unlocked it.

Mom and Rick stood outside, and I walked into their arms. "Mom!"

We embraced, and Rick asked, "Where are your clothes?"

"This is all I have."

He said, "We brought you some street clothes and gave them to the deputy."

After more hugs with them and Raquel and Alex, someone rang the deputy and asked where my clothes were. A little later, he returned with an apology and a bag containing the things my parents had brought.

I couldn't have cared less about clothes. I'd have walked out of the place naked if my skin was all I had. It might have been fitting, because this was like being born again.

I went into the lobby restroom and, for the first time in years, put on street clothes: a T-shirt with a picture of surfboards, and blue shorts.

My parents and I walked out of the jail and into the evening sunlight. Alex and Raquel recorded the moment. I took a deep breath and looked up at the sky. For the first time in my adult life, I felt free.

Alex asked me to say a few words, which I can't remember except that I thanked the California Innocence Project for their work.

The four of us made plans to meet at the courthouse in the morning to get the paperwork for the probation department. I buckled into the front passenger seat of my parents' vehicle. As Rick drove out the parking lot, I gazed around with a heart full of gratitude and a mind filled with wonder.

22

Freedom Unease

Nevada and San Diego

While Rick drove across Pahrump, thoughts and feelings flowed through me like a swirling river. I loved being with my mom and stepdad. I was thrilled to ride in the front seat of a car without shackles or prison garb. But I had gone from almost total sensory deprivation to stimulation overload. The world hit me at light speed.

Rick parked at Walgreens, and he and I got out. The ground felt strange beneath my feet. Everything—even the air around me—felt electrified. As soon as we walked into the store, my senses exploded. Bright lights glared. Colors collided in rainbow beams and ricocheted in every direction. The aroma of candies, fragrance of perfumes, and tang of chemical agents erupted within my olfactory system as if I had just snorted every item off the shelves like a line of speed.

Rick led me down the aisle. "What do you want? Toothpaste and deodorant?"

We stopped in front of a display of dental floss.

"Go ahead and decide what you want," he said. "I'm going to pick up a couple of other things." He hurried off with the cart.

I stood there, looking at row upon row of flossing products. Some were plain, while others came in flavors. Some white, some green, some blue. The floss itself was waxed or unwaxed. Even flosser pick ends came in different shapes. I stood there, staring.

Rick returned. "Just grab anything, Uriah."

When I still hesitated, he asked, "What did you use in prison? Why don't you get something like that?"

I put a package of flossers in the cart, and we checked out. Then we drove to the Best Western where Mom and Rick already had a room.

I sat on the edge of the bed that would be mine for the night. It was extremely soft. I fell back and felt as if I was lying on one of those fluffy cotton clouds you sometimes fly through on an airplane.

I grinned. "This is the most comfortable bed I have ever been on."

We were all eager for my first meal as a free man. But first, I wanted to shower the filth of incarceration from my skin.

The entire process filled me with amazement. This pristine room was a separate bathroom with a door and a lock. It even had an exhaust fan, which I turned on. When I got into the gleaming white shower, I realized I was stepping into it naked and barefoot. So long, shower shoes and not getting undressed until inside a filthy prison stall. And so long, birdbaths over the toilet in a cell. I quickly scrubbed and rinsed off, then stood for a few moments, letting the warm spray of water wash over me. It seemed a ritual cleansing of the evil still clinging to me.

The casino where we decided to eat was a former haunt, and the familiar sounds of slot machines ringing and spitting coins filled my ears. I glanced toward the bar to see if I recognized any of the bartenders, who had all known me well, but was glad not to see anyone I knew.

I decided on prime rib as soon as I saw it listed as a special. Throughout my incarceration, whenever I'd read about animal sacrifices in the Old Testament, it was an all-out assault on my senses, especially my olfactory. I could literally smell the meat cooking and burning on the altar, just like it smelled on the grill when I used to barbecue. My mouth watered and I practically salivated on the pages of my Bible. My plan had long been to begin my freedom by eating meat, preferably beef.

As always, Rick prayed before we ate. He praised God for the day's events and thanked him for the food.

It was a huge meal: prime rib, mixed vegetables, onion rings, salad, and two dinner rolls. It was delicious, and I devoured it all. If I'd been a rag doll, my belly would have burst at the seams.

Back at the Best Western, we embraced each other as we said goodnight. Then I crawled under the covers. The sheets caressed my skin, the pillows cushioned my head. The comforter was thick and heavy and warm.

In the dark, I lay thinking about how amazing this was. I was free.

I am free!

My prayers were groanings too deep for words (Rom 8:26). Only the Holy Spirit could take those unutterable articulations of my soul and offer them as a sweet-smelling aroma to the Father.

Being completely exhausted, I thought I'd sleep. But when I closed my eyes, my mind remained wide awake. My brain blazed hot and bright as the noonday sun, eager to taste and see the world.

Eventually I heard Rick stirring. We sat up and looked at each other in the dim room. He spoke quietly, "You wanna go down and get some coffee?"

It was about 3:00 a.m. when we walked through the outside to the hotel lobby. Lights along the parking lot and sidewalks illuminated the vivid colors of trees and bushes. I smelled the soil, decaying plant life, and different scents emanating from trees.

A delightful coffee aroma filled the lobby, and I put a generous amount of French vanilla creamer into my cup. We sat on soft chairs and talked away a couple of hours and many cups of coffee.

On our way back to the room, the morning sun began to break over Mt. Charleston. When we came in, Mom sat up and smiled at us. We chatted happily together, rejoicing in the wonderful day the Lord had made. Then we packed up to meet Alex and Raquel at the courthouse.

We met and hugged each other in the parking lot. They went inside to get the necessary legal documents, and we all went to the probation office. I signed some papers, and that was it. I was legally permitted to leave the state of Nevada.

The rich dinner and excessive coffee played havoc with my digestive system, and we had to stop so I could use the restroom at Walmart.

Because Pahrump had grown a bit since I last saw it, I asked, "Could we just drive through town, so I can see what things look like?"

We went a couple of miles, but that was enough for me. The more I saw, the more anxiety surged within me. Seeing familiar streets brought back terrible memories of sinful and painful experiences. I needed to get out of that town in a hurry.

We drove to the two-lane highway leaving Pahrump and soon crossed the state line into California. My distress decreased substantially. Every curve, mountain and hill, and every color of the barren landscape was familiar, but it was as if I were seeing it all for the first time.

We stopped for a late breakfast in Baker and then took Interstate 15, which leads directly to San Diego. While my anxiety decreased, the assault on my senses increased. Although I retained cognitive function, it was like a trip on a hallucinogenic drug.

*

When we arrived in San Diego, I was elated. We took the Imperial Beach exit off the I-5 and headed toward home. I had long wondered how it would feel to ride with Mom and Rick on this street, and now my dream came true. For the first time, I saw in real life the house I'd seen in pictures for years.

My parents led me to my room, where I sat on my bed and looked around. Some basic necessities were already there for me, even some things I'd owned before going to prison. And there, sitting on the shelf in the corner of the room, were my books.

We walked a short distance to a Mexican restaurant, and I ordered a favorite drink: *horchata*. After a delicious dinner, which sat well in my stomach, we walked a couple more blocks to the beach.

The ocean's immensity and grandeur permeated my being with a profound sense of mystery. I took a deep breath, filling my lungs with the tang of saltwater and the pungent smell of seaweed.

From day one, I started walking. And I couldn't stop. I loved how I could leave the house at any time, day or night. I loved seeing the beauty of God's creation and the design of men's constructions. My senses feasted on the sights and smells, and I inevitably ended each walk at the ocean, whose rhythmic surf tugged at my heart.

I literally tasted and saw that the Lord was good, but my mind and body couldn't remain at rest. I was compelled to walk two or three times daily. Colors popped, smells assaulted, and sounds reverberated with an intensity that often caused nausea.

On May 8, 2013, only two days after I arrived home, Rick and I drove to Santa Monica for a gathering related to an Innocence March. Justin Brooks, Alissa Bjerkhoel, and Michael Semanchik were walking from San Diego to Sacramento to raise awareness about wrongful convictions, particularly the plight of the California twelve (this number has decreased in recent years, thank the Lord). These wrongfully convicted men and women have no further legal recourse and will remain in prison, unless the governor pardons them or the Lord intervenes in another miraculous manner.

Media covered the event, which took place at the Santa Monica pier. Because I had not yet been legally exonerated, I kept a low profile. The activity overwhelmed me, but I was happy to meet fellow exonerees. The first two I met were Herman Atkins and Eric Volz. Mike Semanchik and I didn't talk a lot that day, but we later became good friends, and he helped me a lot with my adjustment.

I was free, but I was a man without an identity. Only one week after my release, Mom took me to the DMV to see if I could get a California ID.

The lady at the station looked up my record on the computer. "Why don't you just get your driver's license? You didn't lose it; it only expired."

Thank God I had already studied the DMV handbook a bit. I took the test and walked out of the building with a California driver's license. This was a significant milestone that represented independence and freedom.

Because of my previous drug charges, I was still on probation and had to register with the San Diego Sheriff's Department as a narcotics offender. When I came into building and discussed this with a clerk, she looked me up in her computer.

"You're also going to have to register as a sex offender."

I shook my head. "No, I don't. I've been exonerated of those charges."

After arguing about the matter for a few minutes, I said, "I'm not signing any form whatsoever that requires me to be a registered sex offender. I will register as a narcotics offender and that's it."

"I'll be back." She left her desk.

A few minutes later, two detectives came up behind me. "Uriah Courtney?"

I turned. "Yes."

"Follow us."

They led me to an interrogation room. "Have a seat."

One of them crossed his arms. "According to our records, you're a sex offender and have to register as one now."

I repeated the story I'd just told the clerk, but included more details about the evidence that exonerated me. I ended, "I'm not signing any such paper."

The other detective leaned closer and stuck his finger in my face. "If you refuse to sign the paper, we'll just have to arrest you and take you downtown and get all this sorted out there."

My mind reeled at the idea of being hauled back to San Diego Central Jail. All I could think about was how I'd thought I was finished forever with those cold and filthy cells. I'd have done or said almost anything to avoid going back there.

I took a deep breath and tried to collect my thoughts. "May I at least call my attorney? Maybe she can explain things to you guys."

They nodded, and one said, "Yes."

Relief swept through me. When Alissa answered, more relief washed over me. I told her what was going on and handed my phone to the detective in charge. The conversation was short, and he returned the phone to me.

Alissa said, "I will call Brent Neck immediately and get this straightened out."

About twenty-five minutes later, I walked out of the interrogation room with an apology singing in my ears. The head detective handed me his card. "If you need anything or run into any problems regarding this issue again, just give me a call."

I returned to the clerk and signed the narcotics registry form. It took a couple of days for me to recover from that traumatic incident.

But God also filled me with much joy. I had regained the childlike ability to be amazed, and everything inspired awe for the Creator. I frequently looked to the heavens and exclaimed, "God, truly you are an awesome God, and you never cease to astonish me with your glory and holiness."

23

Legal Exoneration

San Diego

Once again, I entered the San Diego County courtroom. My heart pounded. The worst days of my life had transpired in this place, and the DA's office could have decided to make me stand trial again. Sometimes personal agendas or egos stall the advance of truth and justice. But not this time.

Now eager anticipation crowded out my fears and memories. It was June 24, 2013, and this was The Last Court Hearing, the one that would legally exonerate me.

I smiled when I saw Brent Neck representing the State. I respected him for his integrity and cooperation throughout the exoneration process. My personal Angel of Hope, Alissa, sat by me with Justin beside her. Mom, Rick, and Marti (my former prison ombudsman) sat behind us.

"Your honor," Mr. Neck began, "the District Attorney's office will not be re-filing charges but instead, in the interest of justice, dismissing all charges against Uriah Courtney."

The judge read the order: "Upon a motion filed by the San Diego County District Attorney to dismiss the Counts mentioned below, it is ordered that the charge of kidnap for sexual penetration as charged in Count One of the information, and the charge of rape by a foreign object with use of force, as charged in Count Two of the information, be dismissed in the furtherance of justice."

He then read a second order: "In accordance with the dismissal, Uriah Courtney is not required to register as a sex offender under this case. The California Department of Justice and other law enforcement agencies shall update their records in accordance with this order."

That was it. Not only had the physical evidence exonerated me, but now I was legally declared innocent by a judge in the Superior Court of California. Justice, at last, had been served.

Tears flowed from my eyes and praise rose from my soul. From that moment on, I took as my motto the words of Puritan Thomas Brooks: "Truth at last triumphs." God loves truth and will make it triumph in the end, whether we see it in this life or not. I praised him for revealing the truth for all to see.

Mom and Rick embraced me, and we walked arm in arm into bright sunshine and an exuberant crowd of supporters. Many folks from the CIP gathered around to hug us and shake my hand.

Alissa pulled me aside. "A press conference will be held very soon, Uriah, so get ready."

*

She wasn't kidding. The press conference was held the very next day at the California Western School of Law. The thought of appearing before a crowd of people, including news crews, terrified me.

When I arrived, I was surprised to see crews from ABC, NBC, Fox, CBS, KUSI, and more. Mom, Rick, Misty, Justin, Alissa, and Brent Neck sat with me at the front of the room.

Despite my anxiety and struggling through emotional moments, I spoke about my experience and answered the reporters' questions. And I appreciated the opportunity to publicly proclaim my innocence. My voice was finally being heard.

Dad, my stepmom Debbie, and sister Shylee arrived in San Diego that same day. Although I'd spoken with Dad every week or two, I hadn't seen him for seven years. And I hadn't hugged him for almost ten years, so it was wonderful to embrace him again.

Mom and Rick threw a huge party for me on June 30. Nearly all my family members attended, as did most of the CIP attorneys and their families. A few law students, including Alex, showed up. I was pleased to see Jonathan Jordan, the attorney who worked so hard to get me a new trial. My former co-worker who'd testified at my trial and the families of inmates I'd met in prison were also there. We all celebrated my freedom.

At the end of July, Colton and his mother flew to San Diego for a visit. Mom, Rick, Sarah Bear, and Alissa went with me to meet them at the airport. The CIP ladies recorded the moment when Colton and I hugged for the first time in over eight years. We were both a little nervous, and he giggled a bit. But those were the most heartwarming hugs I've ever had. I'd longed to experience this for what seemed a lifetime—actually, it was: Colton's lifetime.

We had only a few days together, but we packed a lot of father-son activity into them. We hiked on pine-covered mountains and dipped our feet in a cold, clear lake. We visited Balboa Park as well as an animal center and marine life aquarium near the ocean. We fished at a large pond, where Colton caught so many fish I couldn't bait his hook fast enough.

And every day we went to Colton's favorite place—the beach. He never wanted to quit swimming, which reminded me of my childhood self. He loved sitting on my shoulders while I waded into the ocean. He was big for a ten-year-old, and it was a struggle to keep from losing him when the surging surf tugged at us, but we hung on to each other.

When we were together, especially if it was only the two of us, it seemed we had never been apart. We cried a little and laughed a lot.

Unfortunately, we've had little time together since. But we enjoyed a brief visit that October and a good visit in Texas in 2015, and we speak regularly on the phone. Although my dream for raising him within a stable and godly family did not become a reality, I hope and pray for more time with him in the future.

You may recall that only two days after my release, I'd participated incognito at the Santa Monica stop of the Innocence March. Almost two months later, many other people and I joined Justin, Alissa, and Mike for the last leg of their 712-mile walk from San Diego to Sacramento.

A man fell into step beside me as our group approached the capitol building. I figured he was involved with the CIP, but I didn't know him.

He asked, "Uriah, what kind of work would you like to do?"

Because I'd been considering that very issue during the weeks since my release, I didn't hesitate to answer. "I'm interested in either electrical work or pipe fitting."

He looked at me. "Really? I happen to have a good friend who might be able to help you. I'll ask him to give you a call."

"That would be great. Thank you very much." I glanced at him out of the corner of my eye. "Do I know you?"

He grinned. "I'm Jan Stiglitz."

"Jan Stiglitz?" *The person whose name topped every list of my CIP attorneys? And here I'd thought all this time that Jan was a woman.*

I grabbed his hand and shook it. "It's great to meet you in person."

A few days later I received a phone call, directing me to a training center for plumbers and pipe fitters, where I took a competency test. Within two weeks, I was working as a pre-apprentice for one of the best mechanical companies in San Diego. I was a mere three months out of prison.

Now I had something to do every day, something I enjoyed. But more important, I could provide for myself again. This job was an important factor in restoring normalcy and continues as one of my life's greatest blessings.

24

Church Home

Santee

Tall palms lined the black asphalt lot. The white church building glowed in the sun, the cross on its peaked roof brilliant against the blue sky. A man stood in front of the doors, greeting and hugging people before they entered.

I swallowed the lump in my throat and walked up. He introduced himself as Bob.

"Uriah Courtney." I shook his hand. "I heard about Christ United Reformed Church while I was in a prison Bible study with the church's deacon, Alex."

"Oh, sure." He smiled. "I know Alex, but he attends a different church now."

If Bob hadn't still been holding my hand, I might have turned around and left. I'd counted on seeing at least one person I knew. And I'd been eager to tell Alex how my innocence had been proven and how the Lord had used him to bring me to this spot.

Bob kept talking in his friendly tones, and somehow I found myself walking through the open double doors. A couple of men shook my hand and identified themselves as elders. Then one asked. "What brings you to our church today?"

My remarkable story amazed them, the word *providence* often rolling from their lips—and those of many others as I told my story over and over that morning. These people were speaking my language. Everyone greeted me warmly, and I couldn't have felt more welcome. I enjoyed everything about the service: the singing of psalms and hymns, the expositional preaching of the Word, the administration of the sacrament—everything.

When I left the building, Pastor Michael Brown greeted me and we spoke. He was delighted that I'd learned about Christ URC through Alex's Bible study and amazed to hear about my wrongful conviction and subsequent exoneration.

Another Sunday, I met Dr. Michael Horton. I could barely restrain my excitement and tried not to treat him like a celebrity. On a later occasion, I showed him the autographed copy of *The Christian Faith* he had sent to me while I was in prison and expressed my great appreciation for his kindness.

I fell in love with the saints at Christ URC, a small part of the body of Christ. I knew without a doubt this was where I belonged.

*

For months, I drove a half hour to attend services. On Wednesday evenings, I took Pastor Brown's catechism class on the Heidelberg Catechism, which I already knew pretty well. After I completed the class, the church elders interviewed me about my Christian faith and scheduled my baptism for November 10, 2013.

My anxiety about crowds skyrocketed when Pastor Brown asked me to stand and answer some questions. But then he baptized me, scooping up water and dumping it on my bent head three times: in the name of the Father, and of the Son, and of the Holy Spirit.

The water flowing down my neck and face seemed to wash away lingering vestiges of prison. When Pastor Brown spoke about my situation, I don't think there was a dry eye in the building. I know mine weren't. That evening I partook of the Lord's Supper for the first time in years.

My pastor, elders, and fellow congregants have enfolded and respected me. Remember my comparison of my newfound faith to having the keys to a new car and being prohibited from taking it out of the garage? These dear saints have been wisely teaching me how to drive my faith car in the world. When I take a wrong turn, they patiently guide me to the right road. When I ignore driving regulations, they gently remind me of the law.

With their help, and that of my family, I gradually adjusted to life after incarceration. Working at a job I enjoyed, speaking for the California Innocence Project, and worshipping with saints who held me accountable. I still belong to Christ URC. I love my church family and thank God for them.

25

Free Indeed

San Diego

I shifted gears as my pickup climbed the mesa. At the top, I parked and got out to look over the edge—down on the sprawling complex of the R. J. Donovan Correctional Facility. A pang of sadness pierced my heart.

So much time lost in that doorway to hell. I thought about my dear brother in Christ, Jonathan, and other souls still languishing behind those walls or in other similar prisons.

For years, I'd hoped and prayed to someday stand on this hill and look down at those yards as a free man. This was that moment.

I took a deep breath. *Thank you, God, for freeing me from that place. And thank you especially for saving my soul from eternal prison.*

It was May 6, 2014, and I was celebrating my first year of freedom.

I walked slowly back to my truck and engaged the gears. Then I drove another twenty-five minutes to the Otay Lakes area. While in prison, I'd sometimes gazed down at these waters, glimmering in the distance, thinking how much I'd like to go there.

Now I parked beside a lake and got out. The prison seemed far away. I filled my lungs with the fresh air, fragrant with eucalyptus. I feasted my eyes on the green trees, brown hills, purple mountains, and blue sky reflected in the still water.

I drove back to town and stopped at a taco shop to eat a burrito. Then I went home and hopped on my old BMX-style racing bike. I rode the sixteen-mile round trip along the Silver Strand, from Imperial Beach to Coronado Island and back. The ocean's salt spray whipped my face.

I was free indeed.

*

Learning to live again in a world filled with temptation isn't easy. If anything, it's even more difficult now that I'm a Christian. The devil is an opportunist who takes advantage of any occasion to put a stumbling block in the path of God's saints.

But he's not completely to blame. Because of our fallen human nature, sin starts in the heart. Being a sinner is easy, but being a saint is far more difficult. Who wants to deny themselves the pleasures of this world and live a life of obedience to God? But Christ alone provides the greatest treasures and the most soul-satisfying pleasures. Although I hold few worldly possessions, my hands of faith overflow with the riches of Christ.

Jesus said, "No one who puts his hand to the plow and looks back is fit for the kingdom of God" (Luke 9:62). I don't want to be the farmer plowing crooked furrows because I'm always looking back instead of straight ahead. I want to focus on Christ, the author and perfecter of my faith.

Am I sometimes bothered that I lost over eight years of my life sitting inside a prison cell, unjustly condemned as a sexual predator? Yes, certainly. Does anger occasionally strike my heart or bitterness seep into my bones? Of course. But God's Word and Spirit pull out those poisonous thoughts before they take root in my soul.

When I'm asked why I'm not angry at the victim and the justice system, I respond that it's because of God working in my heart. I feel sorry and angry *for*—not *at*—the victim. Not only was she raped by a sexual predator, whom the authorities have so far allowed to remain free and under no threat of prosecution, but she also was victimized by the system. She hasn't received justice, her attacker hasn't received the justice he deserves, and in a sense neither have I.

Yes, I'm free and more thankful than I can express, but there's no real closure for the victim or me until the justice system lawfully goes after the actual perpetrator with the same zeal it unlawfully went after me. While I feel this lack of closure, I remind myself that God works all things together for good, and justice is one of his essential attributes. Believing that gives me peace of mind, even when my emotions don't feel peaceful.

Considering how much God has forgiven in my life helps me forgive others. By his grace, I'm able to lay aside thoughts of vengeance, casting anger and bitterness at the foot of God's throne. He replaces thoughts of despair with hope.

Hope that someday my accuser and I might meet face to face, and she'd no longer see me as a vicious monster, but—like her—a victim. Hope that even the man responsible for this devastating chain of events might come to saving faith in Christ. God, and God alone, can break the iron bones of bitterness, and make a stony heart bleed tears of repentance.

If I'm going to plant good seed in straight furrows, I must keep my eyes on Christ.

I was exonerated from the penalty for crimes I did not commit. But we're all sinners who deserve eternal death for sins we have committed. Only those who trust in Christ are free from certain punishment. They are the true exonerees.

Epilogue

God has provided countless opportunities for me to praise and thank him since my exoneration.

Becoming financially independent involved many small steps. First, I had to set up a banking account. But I had no job and only one ID (my driver's license). The bank required two.

The woman I spoke to was kind, but couldn't set up an account without additional documentation or approval. She picked up my application and stood. "Just let me speak to my manager."

Almost immediately she returned with another woman, who smiled widely. "Uriah Courtney, I'd like to shake your hand." The manager turned to the other employee. "Let's help him out any way we can."

She'd seen TV reports about my wrongful conviction and wanted to do whatever she could to help me get back on my feet. There was no longer any question about opening my account.

A few months later, I was able to borrow money to buy my truck, so I could get to and from work each day. Less than a year after starting work, I began the five-year commitment of apprenticeship school. Despite the difficulty of schoolwork, I remain determined to attain my journeyman goal.

Many people are under the mistaken assumption that I received a huge financial windfall after my exoneration. But because the time I spent in prison did not exceed the amount the judge tacked onto my life sentence, I'm not eligible for financial compensation from the state, although most wrongfully convicted persons are.

It took time for me to get a place of my own. With a generous gift from a dear friend and money I'd saved while living with my parents, I was able to purchase a used travel trailer. I parked it next to a fishing lake, surrounded by mountains with biking and hiking trails. Ducks, gulls, and raptors soared overhead. Coyotes howled in the hills. It seemed like living in paradise.

Being on my own was exquisite, but stressful in many ways. The sensory stimuli of buying groceries or other necessities continued to generate anxiety. Even today, shopping or being in a crowd often nauseates me.

Technology frustrated me. I'd always had a somewhat anti-computer attitude, which intensified while I was in prison. But Rick taught me how to use a computer after my release, and I discovered online teaching of my favorite contemporary theologians. Skype and email allowed me to communicate with distant friends and family. Despite a continuing aversion to technology, I used my computer to keep in touch with my attorneys and others I'd met through my involvement with the CIP.

And I became very involved. In April of 2014, Justin Brooks invited me to be the honorary guest speaker at a fundraiser for the Irish Innocence Project.

The Irish Innocence Project? I was intrigued. Although still consumed with anxiety about speaking in public, I agreed.

The fundraiser took place in a fancy restaurant in Balboa Park. The audience consisted of attorneys, law professors, and educators from around the world, including some people from CAPA International and its president, John Christian.

John and I were introduced to each other before the event began, and I confessed how nervous I was about speaking in front of a crowd.

"Don't worry, brother," he said. "I get nervous, too. Listen, all you have to do is be yourself and talk about your experience. It's your story, and no one can tell it better."

John spoke first, and I was impressed with his skill. Then the director of the Irish Innocence Project addressed the audience in an engaging manner. Justin spoke after him, and he was passionate and animated. Then it was my turn.

I'm supposed to speak after these guys? They were great. They're experienced professionals.

I walked to the podium on stiff legs and looked at the room full of elegantly dressed people. They smiled, and I opened my mouth. As I related my experience, my voice cracked and tears ran down my cheeks.

Tears fell from the eyes of some in the audience, too. Others stared spellbound, some holding their hands over their mouths.

After I finished, the people burst into applause and rose to their feet. I tried to work my way back to my seat, but people reached out to shake my hand or hug me. Many of them said they'd never heard such a story. They were shocked something like this could happen.

Someone led me to my chair, but people kept coming over to talk to me. They expressed outrage over this injustice as well as joy that my freedom had been restored.

That night I realized I had been given an incredible platform to proclaim God's glory for all he had done in my life.

In many interviews before and after this event, the question inevitably arose: "How did you get through such a horrible experience?"

I love being asked that question, because it throws the door wide open to speak about Christ and God's glory. While I use my speaking engagements primarily to address wrongful convictions and their traumatic consequences, I almost always mention how God set me spiritually as well as physically free.

Every year, the Innocence Network hosts a conference in a different state. When I attended my first one in 2014 in Oregon, I was amazed to meet over a hundred fellow exonerees.

The accumulated years spent behind bars among all of us were astonishing, sickening. Not only had the lives of the exonerees been devastated, but also the lives of their family members. Hearing their stories was painful, but seeing their faces and celebrating our freedom together was priceless.

Since my exoneration, I've testified at the capital in Sacramento on multiple occasions, including advocating bills for post-conviction DNA testing and new evidence, both of which passed. I've spoken at colleges, high schools, and book clubs, and I am often interviewed.

My friendship with John Christian led to speaking opportunities in Boston, London, and Ireland. I spoke on the toll of wrongful conviction as a keynote speaker at the International Innocence Project Conference in June of 2015 at Griffith College in Dublin.

Peter Pringle and Sunny Jacobs, two married exonerees, invited me to spend a few days at their home outside Galway on the west coast of Ireland. They have set up the Sunny Center Foundation as a place for exonerees to find hope and peace within the context of good food and great friendship.

Even though I'd already been out of prison for two years, I experienced a great deal of joy and healing during this time. Their cottage sat on a rocky hill above a beautiful lake. Old stone fences, erected generations ago, snaked across the green hillsides. Trees, ferns, and flowers covered the countryside in a hundred shades of green. Sunny and Peter were a delightful couple, and I learned a great deal from these two titans of the exoneree family.

In the summer of 2015, I had the privilege of attending Alissa's wedding at—of all places—Convict Lake, California. You can believe the irony of the name was not lost on me. An ex-convict at Convict Lake, witnessing the marriage ceremony of the attorney who helped prove his innocence.

And less than a year later, on June 11, 2016, I married Marina Inez Abdallah.

I'd never imagined the way God would bring my future bride into my life. We met while I worked on a job site at her place of employment. Her black hair, expressive brown eyes, and smile as wide as a rainbow attracted me. But her character was equally attractive. She seemed a real lady and wasn't flirtatious, which I found refreshing and appealing. Our hearts were drawn together from the start.

Shortly after we met, Marina began attending Christ URC with me. This type of worship was a new experience for someone with her Catholic background, but she thrived under gospel preaching that confirmed biblical truths she already knew. After she completed a class in which she studied the Bible and Reformed confessions, she became a member of my church. Then Pastor Brown guided us through an excellent course of marriage counseling.

Marina has become my greatest supporter, my advisor, and my best friend. In every sense of the word, she is my helpmate. She praises my strengths and encourages me to develop them. She recognizes my weaknesses and gently prods me to overcome them. Her good character traits remind me of the Proverbs 31 woman.

God brought not only the two of us together, but also her two children. I love Marc and Sophia as if they were my own kids. I enjoy being a father to them. I would love to see Colton more often, but I appreciate any opportunity I have to be with him.

Marriage isn't always easy because whenever sinners live with each other, there's bound to be some conflict. Nevertheless, being married is an amazing thing and a great blessing. Marina is my wife and my life, the jewel of my heart.

Some stories do have a happy ending. But this isn't the end—it's simply a new beginning where Divine Providence guides the way.

Prison Poetry

Colton

(4-06)

What would it be like to feel your touch?
To hold my son that I love so much.
What would it be like to watch you grow?
To teach you many things that you should know.
What would it be like to see you walk?
To watch your lips as I listen to you talk.
What would it be like to watch you run?
To hear you say Daddy I am having so much fun.
What would it be like to see you cry?
To hold you in my lap while you tell me why.
What would it be like to watch you ride your bike?
To go up to the mountains and take a hike.
What would it be like if you got mad?
To see your face while you're real sad.
What would it be like to hold your hand?
To play all day in the soft warm sand.
What would it be like to see you learn?
To watch you accept an award while you stand firm.
What would it be like to tuck you into bed?
To kiss you good night after a prayer's been said.
What would it be like to just hang out?
To laugh and giggle while we run about.
What would it be like if we went camping?
To sit upon a lakeshore and cast a string.
What would it be like to see you smile?
To play in a park then rest a while.
What would it be like to watch the sun go down?
Sitting with Colton at the edge of town.

Justice in Injustice

(5-13-06)

Open your eyes, Lady Justice, and see
The injustice that has happened to me
Take off your blindfold; let it fall to the ground
Now look at these sowers of corruption; they're all around
Like the detective who planted seeds of lies in the jury's mind
He knew the truth, but he wanted to play the hero instead
Sitting there in his cheap suit and transparent look
It's him who's a criminal; he's a filthy crook
And there sits the witness who wouldn't even stop
He drove right by and didn't call a cop
Another spineless liar who wouldn't tell the truth
That's okay. An eye for an eye, tooth for a tooth
The victim I can forgive because she really thinks I'm the man
But she must have forgot her attacker had curly hair and a tan
That's what happens with time and confusion
Just a jumbled mess like a dream or illusion
Now let me tell you about the prosecuting attorney
If looks could kill, I'd left the courtroom on a gurney
I really thought she was the devil in disguise
There was such contempt when she looked me in the eyes
Now that you see this injustice that happened to me
Be the justice of my cause and please set me free
Put a stop to these sowers of corruption
And make them reap a whirlwind of destruction

O God

(5-18-06)

How long, O God, must I endure this misery?
Caged like I'm an animal under lock and key
My soul cries out to you day and night
Don't stay silent, O God, you've won the fight
Bow down your ear and listen to my prayer
Hold my hand, too, so I know that you're there
How long, O God, must I live with this fear?
I've been bound by these chains for over a year
Come and pull me out of this pit of sorrow
Save me now, O God, I can't wait until tomorrow
You've tested me beyond what I can bear
And still you're silent, like you don't care
How long, O God, will this injustice last?
Remember I'm but a vapor and fading fast
My life is yours, so show me what to do
Guide me, O God, I surrender my will to you
Make all of my enemies run away in fear
And cause me to know that you are always near
How long, O God, will I be an object of scorn?
I feel like you've abandoned me, I'm so helpless and torn
Please don't let me dwell in this darkness forever
But prepare me, O God, for a new endeavor
My patience is exhausted from this overwhelming test
Forgive me, O God. I've given you my best

Thank You, God

(8-22-06)

As I sit upon this mountain ledge
Pondering thoughts of falling over the edge
I'm struck by the beauty of God's creation
The sea that stretches from nation to nation
I taste the salt in the air
As the wind rushes through my hair
God's Spirit floating across the waters
Giving life to his sons and daughters
As I watch waves crash along the shore
I hear them thunder like a lion's roar
A lone seagull cries off in the distance
Taking flight in the currents of least resistance
The tired sun surrenders its mighty light
Shimmering fingers fade away into the night
A calm takes over the restless sea
Bringing an end to its toilsome energy
Lightning flashes across the expanse of the sky
Raindrops fall like tears from angels' eyes
They trickle down the sides of my face
As I look around in awe of this place
I abandon my thoughts of falling over the edge
Thank you, God, for bringing me up to this ledge

Searching

(5-6-07)

As I walk along this path tonight
Shadows dance in the pale moonlight
Like flickering flames they prance around
Creeping about without making a sound
I drift along with these thoughts of mine
Wondering what happened to the sands of time
A whispering wind tells me I'm not alone
Ever searching for a place to call home
Drawing close now, I hear the ocean's roar
Crashing against the cliffs where seagulls soar
The impact shakes the ground beneath my feet
Wave upon wave the rocks get beat
At last I arrive at my special place
Admiring the awesome view before my face
That shadows have all receded into their lair
And my mind has freed itself of despair
I look up at the star-filled sky
A kaleidoscope of color before my eyes
Blanketed by the Great Artist's brilliant masterpiece
Covered with the coat of the Shepherd's fleece
The screech of an owl interrupts my reverie
As it takes flight from a nearby tree
Doubtless searching for its late-night meal
Talons extended ready to make its kill
I'm reminded of a hunger all my own
Endless endeavors for a place to call home
I think for now this spot will do
Because wherever I'm at, God is here, too.

A New Beginning

(5-27-07)

My body was laid to rest long ago
Death was so swift, I didn't even know
To the earth I was returned to dust
My flesh at last could no longer lust
Freed was I from a life of sin
And a wretched body I could not win
Gone was the pain and gone was sorrow
It was a sweet relief without tomorrow
Then all of a sudden, the earth shook
And my dry bones rattled out of their nook
The power of death could not hold me down
When God shook my bones out of the ground
And from out of heaven, his voice was heard
No thunder and lightning, just simply his word
He spoke to my bones and said, "Live!"
"My breath of life to you I give."
Then suddenly sinews and flesh began to grow
Covering my bones from head to toe
With his breath of life breathed into me
He then opened my eyes, and I could see
Looking around now, I was filled with awe
As my eyes adjusted to the things they saw
And I stood upon my feet at God's command
Feeling at peace in this strange new land
Then I was given the whole armor of God
With the gospel of peace, my feet were shod
The breastplate of righteousness covered my chest
To protect my heart while on my quest
With the helmet of salvation over my head
Now I'll follow God's word wherever I'm led
And holding on tight to my shield of faith
The sword of the Spirit will keep me safe

Tears

(8-17-08)

It's been a long while
Since I've shed any tears
Could it be my heart's been hardened
Over the past few years?

Nothing makes much sense
Not that it ever did
Been lost my whole life
At least since I was a kid

Drifting through the years
On one high to the next
Down the funnel of time
My soul severely vexed

I've never been so lonely
Even when surrounded by the past
Alas, these wretched walls
I pray they do not last

So why, you may ask
Would I want to shed any tears?
Well, it's certainly not that
But an overflow of my fears

I can't help but wonder
If perhaps something's wrong
For tears are only human
And it's been so very long

The *Exoneree* Collaboration Story

by Glenda Faye Mathes

When Uriah first used the word *tatted* in our conversation, I envisioned the knotted lace edging on linen handkerchiefs my grandmother tucked into my childhood birthday cards. Uriah (evidently noticing my puzzled expression) explained he meant tattooed.

This anecdote illustrates one of the many ways he and I differ.

It would be difficult to find a more unlikely pair of collaborators. Uriah is a fit young man, and I'm a "mature" woman who's definitely out of shape. Uriah can state the day, hour, and minute of his conversion, while I can't remember a time when I didn't love Jesus and know that Jesus loves me. Uriah's family rarely attended church, was split by divorce, and lived on the West Coast. My childhood family never missed a church service, my parents have been married for over sixty-five years, and I've always lived in the rural Midwest. Although Uriah became rebellious, I was obedient. (At least that's what my mom always said.) He nearly dropped out of school, but I loved every academic minute.

Yet when we met, we felt an immediate connection that superseded all our differences. We are brother and sister in Christ.

How did such an unlikely pair meet and begin working together? The theme of providence runs not only through Uriah's memoir, but also through the story of our collaboration.

It all began with a Facebook status.

On March 5, 2014, Rev. Michael Brown posted, "One of the godliest men I have ever known." Beneath the picture of a young man, he gave a link to a newspaper article about the wrongful conviction and exoneration of Uriah Courtney.

That *San Diego Union-Tribune* story, written by John Wilkens, piqued my interest. A comment by Rev. Brown indicated he'd recently "had the privilege of baptizing this dear brother."

I contacted Rev. Brown, whom I'd met while reporting on ecclesiastical meetings for *Christian Renewal*. I wondered if Uriah might be interested in being interviewed for the publication. About a week later, after checking with him, Pastor Brown gave me Uriah's contact information.

Uriah and I corresponded, and I wrote the article. But before it appeared in *Christian Renewal* (June 25, 2014), I felt convicted that Uriah's story deserved a wider readership. I believed the whole world should read his powerful account of wrongful conviction, painful incarceration, amazing transformation, and extraordinary exoneration. And everyone needed to hear about his ability by God's equipping grace not to harbor bitterness or anger.

On June 1, I emailed Uriah, offering to help him write a memoir about his experiences. I concluded: "But I don't want you to do this unless you firmly believe it's God calling you—not just me persuading you."

Uriah responded within twelve hours. Many people had encouraged him to write a book, which he'd considered but rejected, believing it would be difficult, time-consuming, and of little interest to others. But he promised to pray about it, signing his message: "Glory be to God, Uriah."

Neither of us was sure we should tackle this huge project. Deciding not to proceed unless God convinced us both, we agreed to ponder and pray.

On June 9, I found a picture of Uriah on Facebook. Christ URC had posted a photo showing him greeting a family at his church. As I viewed Uriah, smiling and shaking hands, I knew we should write his story.

That same day, Uriah wrote this:

Hi Glenda,

I've given much thought and prayer about doing a book with you. I've also talked this over with a few people at church, including Pastor Brown, and of course, my parents. Everyone believes that I should take up this wonderful offer. I think so too and have no doubt that it is the Lord's will, for anything that honors and glorifies God would be well pleasing in His sight and according to His will. However, I must confess that such an undertaking causes me much fear and trembling. I am an extremely slow writer and don't feel that I'm very good at it either.

In Christ,
Uriah

As the summer progressed, Uriah sent me chunks of memories that I worked into scenes and chapters. He was a better writer than he thought, but I needed to meet him in person. How could I authentically portray his voice without hearing him speak? I had no plans to travel to San Diego, and—although he had traveled to the East Coast and the Pacific Northwest for Innocence Project events—he wasn't scheduled to travel to the Midwest. In August, I asked him to let me know if he ever had an opportunity to speak anywhere within my driving distance.

About the same time, it became apparent that we needed prayer support. The project seemed insurmountable, and we often felt overwhelmed by spiritual warfare. We discussed developing a network of prayer partners.

On September 22, I received a message Uriah had written the previous day. It said in part: "The Lord bless you, sister. I happened to have lunch today with Kim and Donna, from Kansas, after church today. They said they know you, that you stayed at their house some time ago. What a wonderful connection this is! I met them last year and felt very attracted to them. They are such nice and encouraging people in the Lord."

A wonderful connection, indeed! I had stayed at the Mastalio home in Kansas City one night before flying out early the next morning to report on an ecclesiastical meeting in London, Ontario. I asked Uriah to let me know if he ever visited them in the Midwest because I would happily drive to meet him. I also emailed Donna, catching up with her and Kim and asking if they would be interested in being prayer partners for the memoir project. I mentioned that Uriah and I hoped to meet soon.

Donna responded within hours, saying she and Kim planned to fly to Kansas City the next day and would remain there for the rest of the year, except for "a week at the end of October" when they planned to return for a church conference. Parenthetically, she wrote: "On the off chance you could make it to that conference, we can offer you a guest bedroom here with us, and you could connect with Uriah."

My heart leaped. *Me? Fly to San Diego?* Definitely a matter for prayer. Time to haul in the big guns. I sought Uriah's advice about sending an initial message to our prospective prayer partners and asked about his schedule during that time frame. He gave me the green light regarding both a prayer message and his availability.

I double-checked with Donna to make sure she genuinely meant her parenthetical offer, and she responded positively. My husband encouraged me to go. I checked into flight expenses and considered dates for departure and return. I sent the first message to our prayer partners on the evening of September 25, asking them to pray about a possible meeting and other details related to the work. It concluded with the request "that every aspect of this project will glorify God."

The very next day I received a message from Chris Olow. (While researching dates and information to write this, I realized Chris and his family were the people Uriah was greeting in the picture I'd seen on Facebook.) In his initial message, Chris wrote, "I am a CURC member with Uriah and would like to assist you in meeting with Uriah by offering airline passes to come to San Diego if needed."

I'd quickly gone from having no clue how Uriah and I would ever meet to having a specific itinerary to travel to San Diego, complete with airline fare and a place to stay. It was like God put his hand on my back, gave me a gentle push, and said, "Go, Glenda. Go now."

When I shared this latest development with Uriah, he wrote, "I just love seeing God's amazing providence at work."

When Uriah and I met, we chatted as animatedly as old friends catching up after a long absence. The project surged forward during those few days together. How much easier to brainstorm face-to-face as opposed to sending emails back and forth! Things daily fell into place in such amazing ways that, by the end of our time together, whenever something worked out we'd grin at each other and say, "Providence."

We continued our pattern of email communication for the next nine months, sometimes experiencing lean weeks when the work stalled due to intense schedules or conflicts on one end or the other. But as we neared the last chapters, we felt it was time to work face-to-face again. We needed to nail down some of the legal aspects of the narrative, and it would be helpful for me to meet Uriah's attorney and read his trial transcripts.

Another meeting fell into providential place, and I flew to San Diego in August of 2015. This was a crucial meeting in many ways, but reviewing the transcripts was brutal. The emotional distress physically sickened both Uriah and me. Yet, once again, we accomplished a great deal of work in a few brief days.

Our hope was to complete the manuscript before the end of 2015, and we finished before the end of November. With advice from a publishing expert, we extensively revised it during the first half of 2016. My husband and I flew to San Diego to share Uriah's joy when he married Marina in June. In the fall of 2016, we signed a contract with Wipf and Stock to publish *Exoneree* under their Cascade imprint.

Uriah and I may not speak the same language when it comes to prison lingo or drug culture terms, but we share a common faith vocabulary. I too am personally acquainted with sin's depths and God's vast grace in saving a wretch like me.

Four-year-old Uriah doing what he liked best, exploring outdoors (1983)

Kindergarten (1984)
Wearing the necklace Dad made

Seventh grade (1992)

On top of the Pyramid of the Lost World in Tikal, Guatemala (2003)

Snorkeling in Belize (2003)

Hanging out with nephew Taylen (2004)

Playing with nephews and nieces on beach (2004)

Prison visit from Chaplain and "Mom" Budlove (11-27-10)

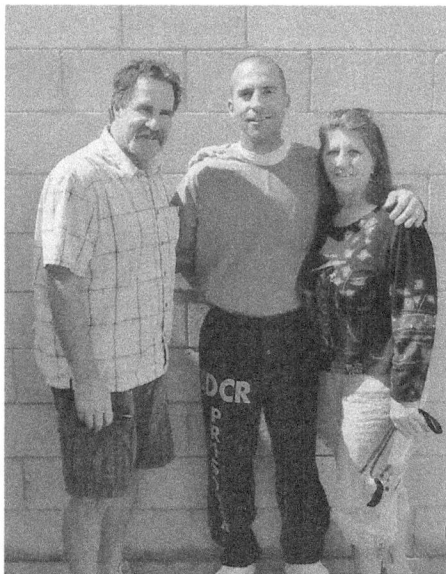

Prison visit from Rick and Mom (4-7-12)

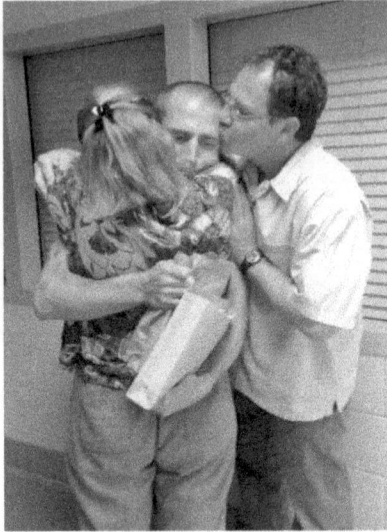

Release embrace (5-6-13)

Walking out (5-6-13)

First post-prison meal (5-6-13)

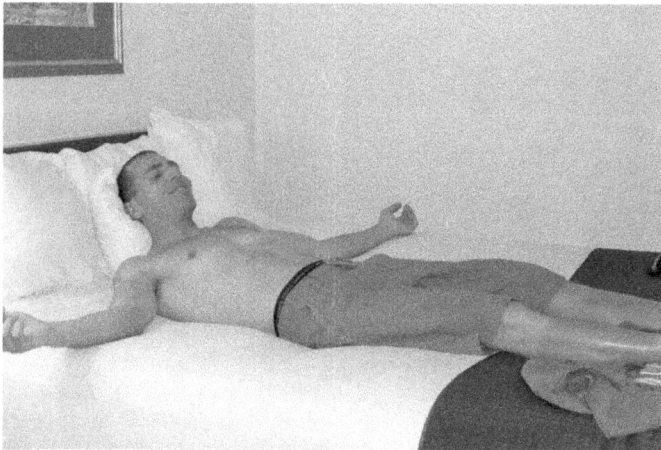

Luxuriating on a real bed (5-6-13)

Justin Brooks speaks at the Santa Monica rally during the Innocence March. On far right, Uriah struggles to handle sensory overload only two days out of prison (5-8-13)

With exoneree Eric Volz at the Santa Monica rally (5-8-13)

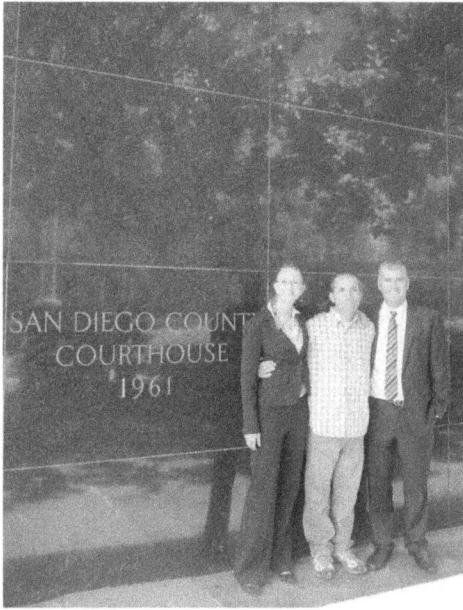

With attorneys Alissa Bjerkhoel and Justin Brooks in front of San Diego County
Courthouse on the day the DA dismissed the charges (6-24-13)

With attorneys, parents, and sister Misty after dismissal of charges (6-24-13)

With attorneys Alissa Bjerkhoel and Justin Brooks at press conference announcing the dismissal of charges (6-25-13)

With Misty, parents, and CIP personnel who attended the press conference (6-25-13)

Uriah and many family members celebrate his freedom (6-30-13)

Uriah celebrating his first post-prison Christmas with Taurus, Rick, Mom, and Misty
(12-25-13)

Speaking on the steps of the capital in Sacramento at the Innocence March reunion
(12-20-13)

Happy exonerees: Tim Atkins, Brian Banks, Obie Anthony, Reggie Cole, Maurice
Caldwell, and Uriah Courtney (12-20-13)

Greeting the Olow family at Christ United Reformed Church in Santee (6-8-14)

Steps to independence: a vehicle and a home (10-30-14)

Living beside a lake provided an important connection to nature (10-30-14)

Uriah writes his memories (10-30-14)

Uriah and Glenda immediately connect when they first meet (10-29-14)

At the Mastalio home (11-1-14)

Uriah with Herman Atkins speaking to incoming law students about wrongful conviction (10-2-14)

Uriah stops in the CIP office and poses with a poster depicting him and Herman Atkins at the Santa Monica rally. Note the contrast in Uriah's facial expression from only two days after his release to less than two years later. (1-15-15)

Exonerees Eric Volz, Uriah Courtney, Sunny Jacobs, and Peter Pringle at Dublin
Castle in Ireland (6-25-15)

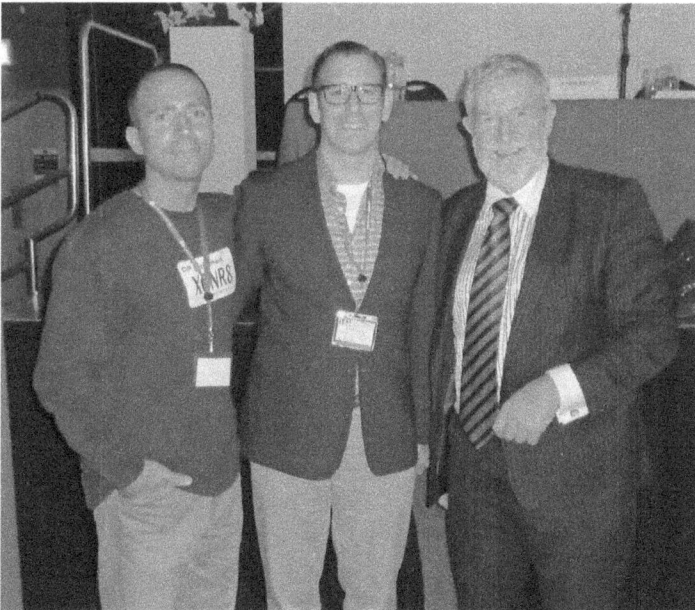

Uriah with John Christian, president and CEO of CAPA International Education, and
Diarmuid Hegarty, president of Dublin's Griffith College (6-25-15)

Uriah and Glenda meet in person for the second time (8-9-15)

At Convict Lake to attend Alissa's wedding (8-23-15)

Uriah and his bride, Marina, with CIP personnel involved in his case: Alissa Bjerkhoel, Alex McDonald, Alex Simpson, Sarah Bear, Raquel Cohen, Kim Hernandez, and Mike Semanchik (6-11-16)

Honeymoon in Belize (6-24-16)

CIP staff, clockwise from front left: Justin Brooks, Ruby Anaya, Audrey McGinn, Mike Semanchik (middle), Alissa Bjerkhoel, Raquel Cohen, and Alex Simpson (6-22-16)

Uriah and Marina at CIP's Taste of Autumn fundraiser with Kim Long, whose murder conviction was dismissed only four months earlier (9-1-16)

With Marina, Marc, and Sophia (7-28-16)

The happy couple (10-22-16)

www.ingramcontent.com/pod-product-compliance
Lightning Source LLC
Chambersburg PA
CBHW030317270326
41926CB00010B/1407